CW00872034

WEIGHTLIFTING TO GROW MUSCLE – UNITED KINGDOM: THE ULTIMATE WEIGHT TRAINING BOOK

Rick Chavarin

Disclaimer

This publication contains the opinions and ideas of its author. It is intended to provide helpful and informative material on the subjects addressed in the publication. The information contained within this book is strictly for educational purposes. The strategies outlined in this book may not be suitable for every individual, and are not guaranteed or warranted to produce any particular results. If you wish to apply ideas contained in this book, you are taking full responsibility for your actions. This book is sold with the understanding that the author and publisher are not engaging in rendering any kind of personal professional services in the book.

The author and publisher specifically disclaim all responsibility for any liability, injury, loss or risk, personal or otherwise, which is incurred as a consequence, directly or indirectly, of the use and application of any of the contents in this book. The author and publisher does not assume and hereby disclaims any liability to any party for any loss, injury, damage, or disruption caused by errors or omissions, whether such errors or omissions result from accident, negligence, or any other cause.

Rick Chavarin

Table of Contents

LEGS BEGIN

<u>Introduction</u>

Weightlifting to Grow Muscle - United Kingdom: The Ultimate Weight Training Book is intended for people who want to build muscle and strength quickly, intelligently, and efficiently. The person may want to compete or create a better body to look better. For some people, weightlifting is part of their physical/mental health and vitality routine, but they want to be rewarded with a better physique as a bonus. This Ultimate Weight Training Book is for the intelligent individual who wants to build the Chest, Back, Shoulders, Arms, and Legs most people can only imagine. The individual who applies these principles will appear as if they compete and have years of professional experience. The routines and exercises are built on the foundation and philosophy of an efficient and streamlined approach to training. Because of this design, zero effort will go to waste, making this book an innovative masterpiece. The methods and strategies will work and are designed for you to customize to your style. Until now, no other book or program has attempted to provide a structure with unlimited variation potential.

Chapter 1: Focused Approach (Chest)

The approach I'm about to teach you is unique. Compared to other schools of thought centered around a go all out, high five, "you can do it," "push yourself," and the usual injury risk approach when training. If you're reading this, you are probably not that person. Maybe you are that person, but you're hungrier than those you train around. You want results! You have the heart to give it your all and be rewarded for it. And you are tired of all the stuff that doesn't work. This book is condensed to get straight to the point without those filler pages. Nobody has time for that. Your training should be efficient, and I hope to encapsulate the same efficiency in every sentence for you.

Efficiency is key, and you'll certainly experience it with this detailed example of an exponential upper chest development process. Of course, common sense dictates you warm up your rotator cuffs and shoulders slightly before beginning this. Still, I'm stating it anyway, just in case. Most people approach the upper Chest with a particular predictable approach. Before anything, they go to the regular bench, if there's one available, and begin to hit those standard sets for 12, 10, 8, and 6-4 Reps. I say if there's one available because it seldom is when you need it. After that, they proceed to an Incline Bench or cable flyes. Are you one of those people? If so, that method won't do much long-term.

I was someone who LOVED benching to the point where I could bench 405lbs. Achieving it took a massive toll on my shoulders. I don't want you to destroy your shoulders, as well. Incline Bench is the better alternative. Regular bench is the cause of most injuries and is the first thing physical therapists recommend avoiding. I wrote this book so you can pursue and attain body composition and development beyond belief in the easiest way possible. Avoiding injury is a big part of that. Less injuries = consistent progress. The Chest portion of this book revolves around Incline Bench, Machine Flyes, and Machine Dips.

Using the principles I will present; you can begin your Chest training with any of those three with any pattern you may choose. For our purposes, we will start with Incline Bench first. I will first show you each step. Then the complete summarized workout set by set.

After warming up your rotator cuffs and shoulders slightly, the process begins with a three-set targeted warm-up, ten reps each set, consisting of the following:

1. Bar only (45lbs)
2. Bar+25lb plate each side (95lbs)
3. Bar+45lb plate each side (135lbs)

The three-set warm-up above applies if you're well trained, experienced, and relatively strong. If you're at a moderate level, then you want to do the following:

1. Bar
2. Bar+10lb plate each side (65lbs)

3. Bar+25lb plate on each side.

If you're a beginner or at a lower strength level, then you want to do the following:

1. Bar
2. Bar+5lb (55lbs)
3. Bar+10lb plates on each side

From here, the initial inclination (no pun intended) for most people is to go for twelve reps, ten reps, and eight reps. They continue this pattern as they increase their weight. They usually shoot for about five sets. This usual approach doesn't do much and is not enough to create any change in your composition. The more effective way to go is by driving your focus towards maintaining muscle memory while building density as you create new muscle tissue. MAINTAIN, BUILD, and CREATE needs to be your mindset. Many people look the same year after year, even after constant training, because they think getting stronger and breaking personal records of strength and reps matters. There is more to it than that.

Getting stronger CAN build the density of the muscle. So as strength increases in the individual, said person might look more prominent. Still, their muscles lack a certain quality—the striations and separation you can see. Building muscle is not just growing. Building muscle is also about creating quality and new muscle fibers to build upon continuously. This book is designed to help you create that quality. The misconception is that cutting will give you that look with those striations due to low body fat. But I want to provide you with a different perspective on the misconception. That look is due to a copious amount of muscle fibers so that you can have that look with average body fat. Therefore, the goal should be to 1) Create new muscle fibers and 2) Grow existing ones and make them denser. Once you achieve those two, maintain with a bit of power training. There are various ways to accomplish this, but I will explain how I do it, and I'm positive this will work for you as well. After your warm-up described above, you want to perform two "Feel" sets and three "Power" sets. The three "Power" sets will be compounded/superset (two workouts back-to-back without rest) with Coffin Presses. You can also achieve the compound set with Dumbbell Flyes or Presses, but my preference is Coffin Presses.

Coffin Presses: These are basically close grip dumbbell presses -- palms facing each other – squeezing the dumbbells together causing the chest to contract as you perform reps.

The "Power" sets will be for mass/density and the Coffin Presses to create new muscle tissue. Keep in mind that the goal for the two "Feel" sets is not to go to failure or even near it. The goal is for your muscles to feel the gradual increase in weight to gauge where your power sets will land. For example, my last warm-up set is at 135lb. My two "Feel" sets would be 5 Reps at 225lbs and 3 Reps at 245lbs. My three "Power" sets range from 255lb-315lb in weight with a 1-3 rep variation. Sometimes I perform my reps in my "Power" set phase in the following pattern: 1 Rep, 1 Rep, 1 Rep. Or 2 Reps, 2 Reps, 1 Rep. Or 3 Reps, 2 Reps, 1 Rep. If you're performing past the four-rep range, then this is your queue to maybe increase the weight on your next training session. Each time is different because different tempos come into play when accomplished. Recovery aspects also play a part, such as nutrition and sleep. Daily individual variation is why personal records to gauge progress are highly unreliable. The actual structure with every set included will look something like this:

1. Bar only (45lbs)
2. Bar+25lb plate each side (95lbs)

3. Bar+45lb plate each side (135lbs)

4. 225lbs for 5 reps (1st "Feel" Set; I can do from 12-15 reps to failure here, maybe more)

5. 245lbs for 3 reps (2nd "Feel" Set)

6. 255lbs for 3 reps (1st "Power" Set; Superset with Coffin Presses using 25lb Dumbbells)

7. 275lbs for 2 reps (2nd "Power" Set; Superset with Coffin Presses using 25lb Dumbbells)

8. 295lbs for 1 rep (3rd "Power" Set; Superset with Coffin Presses using 25lb Dumbbells)

The "Power" sets that are compounded with the Coffin Presses are where you will use The Focused Approach. The Focused Approach begins at the "Power" phase. Each Power rep has a precise rhythm where your breathing is in harmony with the movement. Master this rhythm if you want to reach extreme levels of Power. It would be best if you began to use The Focused Approach when performing your warm-up for practice. Then, continue throughout those feel "Feel" sets, as well. This practice will prepare you for those compounded "Power" sets that will truly change you. If you master that rhythm, you can lift more than most people with your exact body type, years of experience, and weight -- with much less effort.

Focused Approach: Concentrate on breathing rhythm only.

This rhythm is based on a 3 step process and has to be continuous without pausing. The rhythm goes as follows:

1. When your grip is set, inhale deeply before lifting off -- then lift off as you exhale slowly. Do not exhale completely.

2. After the weight is lifted, slowly inhale deeply again as the weight comes down to your upper Chest. Both those actions must have the same rhythm. So when you're at the deep portion of the inhale, the bar must be touching your Chest. Align the movement of the bar and that breathing perfectly. It takes practice, but you will master it.

3. Exhale as you push. The whole process can be done explosively and quickly or slowly and controlled. Your

breathing must match either approach you take. Repeat the rep if necessary using steps 2 and 3.

Practice this rhythm with precision and perfect it. It can be a complete game changer. This type of breathing may yield a paradoxical mindset of relaxation and power and is a part of the structure for consistent progress in strength, density, and mass. Now let's move on to the concept of Chaos to constantly shock your muscles into growth. The Chaos portion is where you will create new muscle fibers to improve your muscle quality and its aesthetic beauty. There are a few ways to make new muscle tissue. The first is: **When the positive movement of the muscle being worked is lighter than the negative portion of the force.** Take a note of that bolded concept. Doing that will create new fibers by ensuring the positive movement (Pushing for Chest & Pulling for Back) & the negative movement (the weight coming down when training Chest) both hit failure at the same time. When doing Coffin Presses immediately after benching, use momentum so the push of the dumbbells feel lighter when you push, and come down really slow for about 7 seconds until they touch your chest. This technique makes the positive movement (the push) lighter than the negative portion of the force (weights coming down). Come down as slow as possible without pausing. If you want to create new muscle fibers to build upon for growth and density, then that's the way to do it. You can apply the same concept to every other muscle you train.

Creating new muscle tissue using the technique mentioned works best with lighter weight. It is light enough to not cause injury and is perfect if you use it as a compound/superset tool right after a heavier Power set using The Focused Approach. The second way to force growth and create fibers is **Blood Flow Restriction**. Make a habit of flexing the part of the Chest you are targeting after every set. Squeeze your chest together and flex extremely hard, giving yourself a well-deserved hug. Flexing in such a way will give you additional development. Squeeze and flex for 10 seconds minimum and max 20 seconds. Arnold Schwarzenegger stumbled upon this neat little hack when he used to flex his biceps after every set. He noticed the bicep he flexed; usually the right one, grew bigger than his left because of that flexing. So he flexed for an extreme squeeze and contraction after every set to give him that additional size with time. The third way is to **Pump More Blood Into The Muscle**. Partials after hitting failure works best. Remember, those three are your Chaos principles to shock for this portion of your upper chest training. I will show you how to apply them in a hyper-efficient and streamlined manner.

The philosophy behind creating Chaos within your structure stems from the majority of people misunderstanding muscle adaptation. People confuse "changing it up" when their muscles adapt to the current stimulus and routine by changing their workouts and exercises. The problem with this habit is most people transition to activities that don't work and practices that work even less. So they're stuck in this cycle of false progress. You want to exploit what works (your structure) and create the Chaos within that structure using partials or changing the timing of how slow you come down on the negative, so muscle adaptation is never an issue, and consistency never breaks. Our success and progress are always linked to consistency or ritual. So keep that in mind because the concept is essential for future chapters. Let's continue with the Chaos portion.

The Chaos portion begins when you have completed your warm-up and your 2 Feel sets. The Coffin Presses will be your Chaos vehicle after every Power set, without hesitation. Or use dumbbell flyes or Regular Dumbbell Presses if you wish. The weight you will be using for your Coffin Presses can range from 10lb Dumbbells to 35lb Dumbbells, depending on how strong or experienced you are. Do not go heavier than that. Remember, you want to use explosive momentum on the push without much effort, to then come down slow on the negative (**When the positive movement of the muscle being worked is lighter than the negative portion of the force**) I prefer 25lbs. Not too heavy and not too light. The purpose of this is to create new muscle fibers. Growing or density is not the focus. Going heavy here is detrimental. Just make sure it is not too heavy and not too light. If you chose 15lb Dumbbells as your baseline, use those 15lb Dumbbells for all three compound sets. Don't increase or decrease the weight. Keeping one set of dumbbells is very important—bringing us back to the concept of structure. Another reason to not increase or decrease the dumbbell weight is due to efficiency. You don't want to do your Power set (for mass & density), compound with coffin press, finish, walk to get dumbbells of different weights, then walk back to the bench. EVERYTHING we do to make your transformation process successful has to be efficient and streamlined with no wasted output. Don't get cute, and don't waste time.

Here's how I get this done: Before anything, I set up a set of 25lb dumbbells for the Chaos portion next to me. After my three warm-up sets and two Feel sets, I increase the weight to 255lbs to perform my first Power set. I lift off and perform 3 Reps using The Focused Approach with the precise rhythm I described. Breathing precisely is your main priority. Next, I grab the dumbbells and perform my Coffin Presses with the number one way to create new muscle tissue— **the positive movement of the muscle being worked is lighter than the negative portion of the force**. You use your body's momentum on the way up, without jerking, and slowly come down for 7 seconds with the upper part of the dumbbells touching your lower Chest. The Coffin Presses will also be performed on the incline bench for efficiency purposes once again. This compound process is a continuation of The Focused Approach, but here's the kicker. You do not count your reps when using your dumbbells. You only focus on the movement. The momentum to make the push lighter – then the really slow negative! Your set ends 3 Reps AFTER it starts to burn. Count your reps for Power set and don't count for Chaos with dumbbells. That simple.

Everyone you know that lifts lack progress because they tell themselves, "I want to shoot for X amount of reps." The issue is that your brain and body give in around that limiting goal you gave yourself for reps. A limiting mindset is not you, though. You're different and go beyond. After your compound set is complete, extreme flex your upper Chest for 10 seconds to add the blood-flow-restriction Chaos principle for that ultimate one-two punch. The beauty of that powerful flex is to fill a gap of satisfaction with your set. Suppose you feel your Power set compounded immediately with

Coffin Presses was not enough to satisfy that sense of completeness. Maybe you feel tired that day so you couldn't do that many reps (even though you're not counting) In that case, you can flex harder and longer instead of doing extra unnecessary sets as most people do. Ok, so that covers the first compound/superset. Let's move on to the second.

For the second compound/superset, when we increase the Power portion of the set, we could do the same thing and follow the same process. Then continue with the third compound set and do the same thing again. It's totally fine to go that route. I occasionally exploit the sets and do the same thing for all three if I feel the pumps/intensity justify it. We want to exploit what works and discard what doesn't. Those three compound sets would be enough for you to change your body composition to a moderate level. But we're not done yet, though. We want to be at a very high level! We can still add one more chaos principle to this dynamic—**pumping blood into the muscle**. We accomplish this by adding partial reps to the Coffin Presses in the third set.

Remember the part when I told you to add 3 Reps after it starts to burn? Instead of performing those 3 Reps, perform 10-20 partial reps, about a quarter movement closest to the Chest. If you end up going with the partial reps, you don't need to flex after the set is complete. Doing so becomes redundant. With more experience and practice, you'll be able to create many variations with these principles. As your experience increases, your creativity and the variations harmonize with your style. I'll end this chapter with a revelation of a happy accident when you go through The Focused Approach. The revelation is this. During those Power sets, we weren't too concerned about strength increase. Your strength will increase exponentially without you even focusing on it. You won't even need to attempt to make progress with power and strength. Indirectly, power and strength will increase when you master all these principles.

Workout Routine Summary

Sets 1, 2, & 3: 10 Rep Warm-Up for Each Set. Get in tune with your breathing Focused Approach.

Sets 4 & 5: Moderate-Heavy weight "Feel" sets. Be able to perform 3-5 reps without reaching failure. The purpose is to maintain The Focused Approach breathing pattern with harder to manage weight. This will prepare you for heavy Power sets.

Sets 6, 7, & 8: Heavy weight Power sets using The Focused Approach breathing, then quickly superset with Coffin Press, Dumbbell Flyes, or Dumbbell presses using light weight (keep one set of weights next to your bench). Don't count reps and only focus on momentum for the push, and slow negative. Stop 3 Reps after it burns, or beyond, for sets 6 & 7. At the last set add extreme partials to finish off.

Note: You can use the same process for regular flat Bench Press.

Chapter 2: Indirect Approach (Chest Cont.)

The importance of goal setting in everyday life is the foundation of success. In our finances, education, career, and relationships, we must have a goal to gauge where we are currently. It can also guide us to get a clear idea of where we're going. I'm sure you have achieved some goals you have set for yourself in the past and automatically felt proud about it – as you should have. You had a target, and you hit it. Joy and confidence are inevitable when you embody that sort of competence. Unfortunately, the same very valuable goal-setting mindset can be detrimental when building the body you want. The detriment indicated is a massive shift for most people and very hard to wrap their head around. A practical mindset for everyday life can be an anchor for what you're meant to become physically. Unfortunately, goal setting holds you back in your muscle-building endeavors.

The natural inclination in the pursuit to transform our body is to have the same goal-setting mindset we have for most things. The philosophy mentioned above is a limiting system for improving physically. You CAN make significant progress by having a goal and tracking things constantly. Such a pursuit can be very daunting and requires a disciplined mind. Even with such discipline, the results for most people are subpar. You're reading this book because you are not most people. You want better results most efficiently. Discipline and tracking play a tiny part in pursuing what we do. So pay attention because this mindset shift is very valuable and helpful. Let's say you do reach your physical goal. A short-sighted plan most people have. They want to lose weight for a wedding, summer, or something. Let's say you lose those pounds. Let's say you get bigger biceps. Or you get stronger. There are two directions you can go from there in each area after you achieve them. Obviously, you can lose more weight or gain more weight. But losing too much weight can become highly unhealthy, and gaining weight leaves you back at the beginning. Sometimes you gain a lot more weight, making you heavier than you were previously. That's usually the case for most people because maintaining doesn't spark joy. The person loses weight. Then they fall back into their old ways, and the body gains more fat out of necessity due to perceived future depletion. The body thinks it will be depleted once again, so it holds more fat at a more rapid rate. Then the weight becomes harder to lose. Weight loss programs require an overhaul of a person's lifestyle. This book is based on strategically incorporating training principles into your current lifestyle. You will indirectly lose that weight if there is weight to be lost.

Ok. So let's say you get the size biceps you want -- but remember that if you grow them too much, out of proportion to the rest of your body, they might not look good. There's also the ideal ratio for shoulder size and Tricep size to accentuate the Bicep properly. So then, the goal for most people becomes maintaining them at the

32

perfect size where the proportions are aesthetically pleasing to the eye. "Maintaining" to me is a virtuous form of giving up. Consistent, never-ending progress will never fail you, so that needs to become what you strive to accomplish. Anytime you make your goal "maintaining," the setbacks pile up. So always strive for progress one way or another. Try to maintain your size as you improve other Bicep areas indirectly. The biceps have other distinctive areas you can strive to improve when an ideal size is achieved. You can seek lower bicep development. You can develop the peak as well. You can also increase vascularity. Plus, you can create new muscle fibers – making those areas of improvement much easier to achieve. There is ALWAYS something to improve or transform.

Now let's say you get stronger. You get that high when you push the limits of your strength. Then you want more. Such a pursuit becomes a cat-and-mouse game of progress and regression. The strength-gaining process usually plays out that way. Strength-obsessed individuals fall into this trap. Trust me. I was one of them at some point. Pursuing power and strength are not endeavors where patience as a virtue applies. Inevitable downfalls in pursuing power and strength can lead to crushing setbacks some people never recover from. An obsessive mindset in pursuing only strength comes with its problems.

The problem is associated with your joints and tendons. Your joints and tendons won't allow the rapid progress you crave because they haven't had the time necessary to adapt. Another set of problems includes a slight wrist injury, elbow injury, or shoulder injury. More reasons why a constant strength-gaining mindset is not viable in the long run. In Chapter 1, I showed you how to indirectly increase strength without putting your shoulders, wrists, and elbows at significant risk. There is always a risk, but risk needs to be minimized for long-term success. The only consistency to a stubborn strength-gaining mindset is injury. When you have to backtrack your training due to injury -- and that strength you gained goes along with it – you have to start from square one to get it back. You proceed forward and then backward. This cycle continues and becomes part of a person's training style. Then you get older with lingering injuries. From that point on is all backward. Change the mindset and indirectly increase your strength safely using the chaos principles. Longevity is vital because there is always an after. Stick to The Focused Approach for power and strength but ensure strength gain does not become your principal mindset.

I always regressed when I had strength as my primary mindset and became my primary motivation. I got to the point where I was benching an ego-driven 405lbs when I weighed 190lbs. It was a bit ridiculous and highly unnecessary. I had a process to reach that level of strength. I used a combination of powerlifting and bodybuilding principles structured uniquely. I thought nothing could stop me. Then, one day I injured my shoulder, and even benching a measly 225lbs for one rep became a struggle. My shoulder injury was a very humbling experience. Of course, it was very depressing, and I took a few weeks off to have a pity party. Little did I know it was a blessing in disguise.

Because of that, I had to change my training and become more efficient and balanced. I'll tell you one thing: My chest and shoulders look better now than they ever did when I was benching the amount mentioned before. Focusing on what makes muscles grow exponentially and how to create more muscle tissue simultaneously became my obsession. I would say that most people who train are stuck in a hopeless loop without realizing it. There is a false progress loop when attempting to get stronger. It also happens when you pursue a short-lived goal using a finite mindset. This limited mindset inevitably leads to some regression when an injury occurs. What you want to pursue is constant, joyful, and never-ending progress. Focus on minimizing injury. You must also recognize how strength and power are about 10% of muscle growth and development. The constant injury becomes your territory when you live in that 10%. Seeking power and strength must be approached with wisdom and a certain level of respect. So let me show you the alternative. This alternative to strength gain as a primary focus is The Indirect Approach.

The Indirect Approach is a bit abstract. The best definition I can give you is this: There's an indirect benefit to multiple, unrelated areas when the focused action is in one primary area. Doing one thing benefits other things. Progress is constant if you can manage to include copious methods where indirect benefits exist in your training. Chapter 1 had a few indirect benefits for the practices described. And many more are to come. I will explain further as I teach you a new method for rapid growth and strength gain. This method is called The Power Bomb and is performed in one very long set. If used correctly, this method will activate exponential growth and include other benefits.

METHOD: POWER BOMB

Sometimes we don't have the time to get an ideal workout in. We need to get it done. There are other times when we are ready to train. Still, we don't have that emotional or mental margin to concentrate on The Focused Approach or other focused-based chaos principles. Sometimes you don't have the time to get all philosophical about things. That's when this method comes into play. This method is one of those intensity-based principles. It serves as a very effective tool for rapid muscle development. It doubles as a productive shortcut and as means to ensure nothing was left on the line. Doing this method I'll soon described, after the sets performed in Chapter 1, will almost guarantee growth and strength on a weekly basis.

During incline bench, we managed to exploit the structure and create chaos to disrupt adaptation. After the incline bench -- we will jump into Machine Flyes -- not Cable Flyes -- for the ultimate shock to the chest. You can do Cable Flyes but this works best with Machine Flyes. At this point, The Power Bomb Method will come into play. This method sounds super cool. That's because it is! The Power Bomb will rapidly expose your muscles to the type of growth many people dream of. It's incredibly effective when performing Machine Flyes. Think of this method as a sort of shortcut to fiber creation. But it must be done correctly and executed at certain times to be effective. Remember that this method is not a substitute for our previous methods. This method pumps a lot of blood into the muscle and has other functions, bringing us back to one of our Chaos principles from Chapter 1.

The Power Bomb Method is essential for an indirect approach to training. Besides pumping blood into the muscles – this method also depletes glycogen levels at a rapid rate. A similar effect to being on a low-carb diet overtakes the body, inadvertently increasing your fat-burning capabilities. Another indirect benefit is the rapid increase of mitochondria – the cell's powerhouse, making it easier for you to burn fat and use energy properly. All of these are requirements for reversing insulin resistance. Insulin resistant people tend to gain and retain more fat. But most importantly, it creates new muscle tissue as well. The new muscle tissue gives you that ripped look you can accomplish without your body fat being low. So indirectly, we achieve various things without them being our primary goal. Well, isn't that neat! Make a habit of adding this method to your Chest routine at least every other week.

The way we begin this is relatively straightforward. We adjust the seat position according to what area you want to target on your Chest. If you're going to develop the upper chest more, put your seat all the way down with hands aligned with your upper chest. If you target the middle chest, place the seat in the middle with hands aligned on your middle chest. If you want to target your lower chest, put the seat at its highest with hands aligned at your lower chest area. Use this as a chance to develop your intuition. Figure out your precise hand position on the handles, seat position, and where exactly you feel the muscle being targeted according to your adjustments. Once you get this down, then we proceed with The Power Bomb Method.

Traditionally, The Power Bomb Method begins with the lowest weight possible on a machine. You don't want to do this with weights since changing them constantly is not very efficient or optimized. Use machines for any Power Bomb Method usage. There's too much lag time in between using weights– time wasted that could have best been used getting through more sets. Many people fail to realize this, so their workouts take too long, and as a result, those workouts become inefficient. If they take too long because of long setup times, this can lead to a catabolic state in which the muscle breaks down. Maybe they train the appropriate amount of time, but the workouts are again inefficient due to long setup times for their set. Remember that your movements must be efficient and streamlined without prolonged wasted setup times. Don't be one of those people who spend 2 hours at the gym but only train for about 20 minutes because you're constantly wasting your time setting up complicated workouts. Be there for almost half that time, or a bit past that. And work out about 80% of that time—just food for thought.

The Power Bomb Method starts by performing 10 Reps at a light weight in the machine. You then move up one level in weight (make weight heavier), perform ten reps again, move up another level in weight for 10 reps, and so on. This pattern continues until you can't do ten reps anymore. When you can't do ten reps due to muscle failure, you lower the weight level one by one performing 10 reps. You perform ten reps on every level going in reverse until you can easily do ten reps. The key term here is easily doing ten reps. When you're able to do ten reps easily – that's when you stop. You do not go past the ten rep point even if you can. The traditional way of doing this method is pretty impressive, but it is not fully optimized for maximum efficiency. I must address a few issues with this way of performing The Power Bomb Method. After I address those issues, I will give you its improved, optimized version. This enhanced version will ridiculously transform the composition of whatever body part you use it to target.

The traditional way worked wonders for me, but my muscles adapted quickly. At first, my muscles would give out around my 7th set on the increased level portion of the process. On my 6th set, I could do ten reps. I would increase the weight level quickly and perform about six reps on my 7th set. Now it was time to reverse the weight. I could only do about 3 or 4 more sets as I lowered the weight performing as many reps as I could for each set. I would hit ten reps on the 4th set on the way down and ultimately stop even if I could do more. The straightforward process satisfied the requirement for The Power Bomb Method. Not too bad! The pumps were crazy, and the change was astonishing.

I struck gold, I thought! After a week or two, I saw a massive improvement in my chest development. I was in shock as to how well my muscles responded. I used this for Biceps also. That hurt like hell. One day I went back to train and suddenly began to have a good problem. I did not notice this the first time. I saw it weeks later. Every time I did The Power Bomb Method – I was able to hit ten reps quickly after I lowered the level of weight only once. It took one set!—not 3 or 4 like before. My muscles recovered way too soon as I decreased the level of weight. After that, I started to make a mistake, my own way of adapting to my good problem. To solve my immediate recovery problem, I began performing reps until burnout, past the ten reps on my set leveling down. I did this to feel the same effect and pumps I felt previously. Going for more reps until burnout was a colossal mistake. Something didn't feel right when I began doing it, but I continued anyway. Have you ever come across this? Do you continue on a path you know you shouldn't with the hope of a positive outcome?

Due to burning out, I soon began to lose size rapidly. Unfortunately, I was burning out at the wrong time. Burning out put me in a catabolic state. I was pushing myself, in a bad way, to the point that my workout became ineffective. For The Power Bomb to be effective, your muscles need those few seconds of rest from when you finish a set, change the level of weight, then begin the set again. Those seconds are precious and required. The improved version fixes the quick recovery issue for continued use once your muscles adapt. Each time you perform The Power Bomb Method, it will be just the right amount of activation and output for continued gains. I suggest you begin with the traditional way for the first few weeks, then move on to the improved version once you feel that adaptation I just described. The recovery will tell you when the time is right.

The Improved Power Bomb Method begins with a few levels above the lowest weight, not the lowest like before. It needs to be light enough for you to do 20 reps or more efficiently. Just by looking at the weight, you should know what that is. Don't overthink it. Pick a few levels above the lowest and get started. Begin the same way as the traditional method described before. Perform ten reps, one level up, ten reps again, and one level up. Instead of lowering the weight to the point where you can't do ten reps anymore, continue until you can't perform five reps. Contract and hold for 10 seconds on that last set on the way up. So it will look like this:

- **<u>Example Power Bomb Set:</u>** Put weight slightly higher than the lowest, perform 10 reps, level up quickly, start 10 reps quickly, level up, 10 reps, level up, 9 reps, level up, 7 reps, level up, 4 reps with a 10-second contraction hold at the end of the 4th rep. Then reduce the weight level, 5 reps, level down, 6 reps, level down, 8 reps, level down, then stop at 10 reps even if you can do more. That's it! You're done.

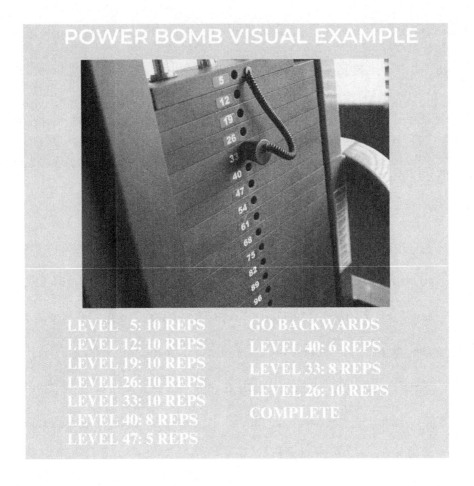

You can also use The Power Bomb Method for dips on a dip machine, emphasizing your lower chest and not your triceps. Use the methods I have shown you to create variations for your Chest routine. These are a couple of my variations, so you get a clearer picture.

Use these principles to maximize your gains. I will give you two variations only. Come up with your own and build on those two:

- o Variation #1 for Complete Chest Routine:

  1. Incline Bench (The 3 warm up sets, 2 Feel Sets, and 3 Power Sets Superset with Dumbbells)

  2. Machine Flyes (Power Bomb)

- o Variation #2

  1. Bench Press (The 3 warm up sets, 2 Feel Sets, and 3 Power Sets Superset with Dumbbells)

  2. Dips for Lower Chest using a Machine Where you Sit down (The Power Bomb Method)

  3. Incline Bench (Focused Approach Only for 3 Power Sets; No Superset or Coffin Presses or Chaos Principles; Just 3 Sets)

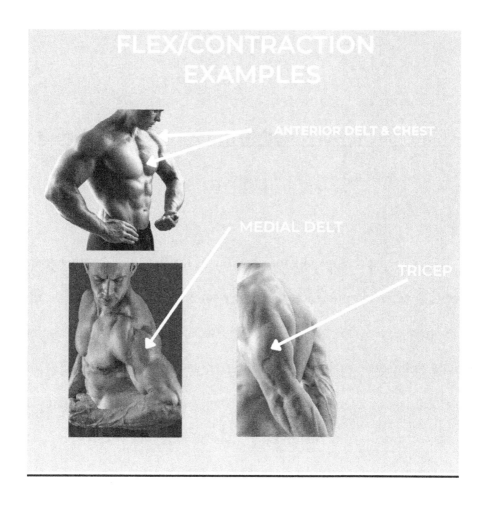

Chapter 3: Body and Mind Connection (Front Delts)

The focused training will inspire you to hit those sets with higher efficiency and confidence. The effort is minimal because your desire for progress will be greater than the work you put in, to the point where any work feels overshadowed by such passion. A state of effortlessness even when work is being done gives it a minimal sense at times. With this in mind, this book is most likely the most minimal approach out there made for a unique type of person. That type of person is usually both driven and lazy. Efficiency is clever laziness. For those people who have those two unique personality traits, this book is a real treat. The effort it takes is also exceptional.

It takes a lot of emotional, peaceful energy but simultaneously increases those emotional reserves, set after set and day after day. So it takes a lot but also gives you more. Then it compounds after you're done.

Next thing you know, the issue becomes stopping your consistent training and taking a rest day. But, of course, you won't want to—a fantastic problem to have indeed. You've most likely heard about the body and mind connection. Pros talk about it, and competitors of every discipline know how important it is. I believe it is THE MOST crucial part of training specific to weightlifting. This book was built with the body and mind connection at its core. But, such a mindset goes much, much deeper. The mindset is not an intelligence exercise or something genetically gifted people have. Body and mind connection is a skill that can be honed and refined, perfected, and constantly transcended—honing that a higher level of body and mind connection requires you to change your mindset and approach when training.

To achieve it, you must give up your initial motivations. Going to the gym to impress or get specific results with a goal-setting mindset will prevent you from achieving this. Such thinking becomes a distraction when trying to achieve Body and Mind Connection. Even the you vs. you approach falls short. You know what I mean—those people who compete against themselves for some reason. The worst form of motivation is looking good for a season, usually Summer. If that's you, that Summer person, give that motivation up. With this process, you'll have a Summer body every winter, as long as you hone this higher level of body and mind connection. Look inward and focus, never outward. Achieve that state of total euphoria and peace as you have a perfect rep, then a perfect set, then a perfect training day. Destroying one's body with all-out workouts to feel accomplished is the manic way of training. Such training is for below-average lifters. This type of training is not for you because you strive for greater heights. You must separate the old from the new to become your entity because you are unique.

Separation in the shoulders is highly coveted and challenging for lifters to achieve. Lucky for you, I will explain a simple and streamlined way to accomplish this. The Chapter 1 concepts will come into play, refining your understanding of The Structure and Chaos Principles discussed before. The setup needed is relatively simple and efficient. As you can tell, simplicity and efficiency are common themes throughout this book. Efficiency compounds progress. So always think about efficiency. When you deviate and start getting too extra, go back to efficiency every time.

We begin our shoulder separation journey with an Overhead Shoulder Press Machine. It can be either plate loaded or one with a pin to increase or decrease the weight. You also need one set of dumbbells, 10lbs only, to do front raises as a compound movement after every shoulder press set. This compound setup is the same one we used when we initially targeted the upper Chest on the incline bench. With time you will increase the dumbbell weight as your muscles adapt. Don't increase the dumbbell weight once you pick which ones you want to work use. Refer to the concept when Coffin

Presses was added as a compound movement.

This setup needs to be in place soon after completing Chest. All you need is three sets for this to work. That's it! There is no warm-up and no feel sets. Previous Chest exercises will warm up your shoulders, so there is no wasted time. Such transition is essential because you'll exploit efficiency each time you move on from one workout to the next. The transition after Chest works as follows:

1. Shoulder Press with Moderate Weight to Failure as your Structure Superset with 10lb Dumbbell Front Raises using Chaos Principles.

2. Shoulder Press with Moderate to Heavy Superset with 10lb Dumbbell Front Raises using Chaos Principles.

3. Shoulder Press with Heavy superset with 10lb Dumbbell Front Raises using Chaos Principles. Not much more is needed. This compound set works because the Incline Chest portion from Chapter 1 will indirectly work out your shoulders to a very high degree. This portion fills that gap to finish them off. Again, you don't need more.

Where the Body and Mind Connection comes into play is on those raises. You must adjust your body and the angle of the raises until YOU feel your form is correct and you're isolating. The burn and pump will tell you. Just think of them as clues. You must pay attention to the ideal burn your muscles feel and the intricacy of the pump. One will tell you if you're on the right track within your workout, and the other will tell you after. You can watch hundreds of YouTube videos on "proper" raises, but you must find those angles to hit those sweet spots.

Add partials on the movement's lower or upper portion, contract, hold, and adjust the range. Try new ways of attacking it. Just don't do anything silly or extravagant that may cause injury. Please keep it simple and focused. Practice those angles with the selected dumbbells. When you find the correct angle where the burn is unique in a good way, and the pump is unlike anything you've felt, you must exploit it and grow. Please keep returning to it, improve on it, and continue to control it as you make the movement yours. It's quite a fun thing to figure out. When you finally figure it out, you'll be unmatched regarding technique. Then you'll be able to apply that body and mind to other parts in very creative ways to make each movement yours. Here's a summary of your current training process:

Chest	Front Delts
Workout #1: Incline or Regular Bench with Dumbbell Superset Process	***Workout #3:*** 3 Sets for Shoulder Press Superset with Dumbbell Front Raises
Workout #2: Powerbomb Machine Flyes, Cable Flyes, or Lower Chest Dips on Machine.	

Chapter 4: Simplicity Approach (Side Delts)

In this chapter, I will show you how to sequence The Simplicity Approach to grasp a level of unmatched sophistication in your training. Keeping things simple opens the door to recurring mastery using repetition– because repetition is the mother of aptitude and skill. The day-in and day-out precise repetition others lack will become the bedrock of your marginally superior skills compared to theirs. The following is a quote I want you to preserve in your engagement with this chapter. I hope that it will guide you through this section and throughout your future transformation methods:

"The trouble with so many of us is that we underestimate the power of simplicity. Any fool can make something complicated. It takes a genius to make it simple" – Albert Einstein.

Targeting your shoulders with dumbbell raises, the middle head, to be more specific (Or Side Delt), requires a ridiculous amount of precision and mastery. Such a need for precision is where the constant disappointment originates from in the quest for those superior shoulders. I frequently observe individuals undertaking the challenge of the dumbbell raises inappropriately, or sometimes acceptably, but with an erroneous emphasis. I will assist you in resolving those errors while exercising a better alternative. For the foreseeable future, defer lateral dumbbell raises until you achieve a level of mastery using the Lateral Raise Machine. Once you master the Lateral Raise Machine, a deep understanding of targeting the middle head of your shoulders will be inevitable. You will develop your middle deltoid any way you aspire to without restriction. There are several reasons why you ought to defer dumbbell raises until

your understanding regarding the feel of your mid-shoulder is innate.
Here are the reasons:

1. Your middle deltoids activate best in the first quarter of the movement. The issue with dumbbell raises stems from activation taking place halfway through the exercise – which is already a failure in the technique. There is hardly any activation past the first quarter of the movement and beyond because the traps start getting involved. Ideally, having your elbows tucked in should be your default. From here, you initiate the action to push outward, keeping tension at the beginning of the movement. Not 5% into the move because it has to be at the beginning.

2. Let's say you're standing relaxed, holding your dumbbells as they touch the side of your thigh. This stance is already a failure in the technique once again. The dumbbells, in that fashion, puts you about 20% into the movement necessary to activate. Most people do not realize this mistake. It would be best if you tuck your elbows into your armpits. There is too

much space from the thighs to where the beginning of the movement should be.

3. There is a weight restriction due to your wrists. Without even considering the range of the movement we discussed in #1 and #2, you need decent weight to get proper growth and development on that shoulder. When you jump into 25lb+ territory, the predisposition for most people is to use momentum to get the weight up. Unfortunately, the wrists also tilt down involuntarily, so there's even less activation throughout the movement. That whole process is a complete disaster from start to finish.

4. There is also the impingement issue (triggering the shoulder to hurt with that pinching sensation). The painful problem happens when you tilt your wrists slightly as if pouring into a tea cup from a kettle. Unfortunately, this practice is prevalent and often used to develop proper contraction. Such a practice ought to be avoided.

LATERAL
MACHINE RAISES

The lateral raise machine solves ALL of these concerns if performed as instructed. You will ensure some of the best competition-level shoulder development out there. The machine solves the initial movement activation problem, perfectly working through the first quarter of the movement. It solves the weight restriction problem, allowing you to go heavier as desired. And ultimately solves the impingement issue as well, not needing to tilt the shoulder unnaturally, which may cause injury. You keep control the whole time when you use the machine. The previous Chest and Front Delt Overhead Shoulder Press (Anterior Head) exercises indirectly required a high volume of involvement from the middle head of the shoulder. Not enough to create growth and development, but just enough to get rid of a prolonged warm-up and a few sets you would have otherwise wasted time on. You will only need one little warm-up set and 3 Maximum working sets using some Chaos principles. You can also go The Power Bomb Method route to knock it out in one very long set. Let's commence with a few missteps to avoid when exercising the lateral raise machine:

1. **Avoid placing the pads across the bicep area or the higher part of the elbow across the forearm:** Many people put the pads too high on the upper portion of the elbow near the bicep area. Placing the pads this way will involve the traps too much

and initiate the tension past the quarter range movement needed for proper activation. Instead, the pads need to be closer to the lower part of the elbow. Therefore, when the activity is initiated, there is tension right away. Again, the seat position must be a bit high to achieve this.

2. **Avoid resting the arms next to you:** Tuck in your elbows under your armpits slightly and lean forward slightly as well. Not too much. The slight lean and tuck will give you the initial tension required and the natural movement of the shoulder, getting rid of that impingement issue.

The Simplicity Approach is a potent tactic to streamline and optimize your routines. I have been very detailed about targeting the middle head of the shoulder the proper way to the point where it can seem a bit overwhelming. But there's no need to be overwhelmed by all the instruction. Sit down, put the seat up high, tuck in your elbows, lean slightly forward, and begin the reps without going higher than shoulder level. That's it! Please keep it simple. I will present the Chaos Principles that are most effective for the task. But there's no need to get lost in all those details I described before. Those explanations are there, so you have a deeper understanding of why we do what we do. The understanding is the difficult part. The doing is a piece of cake. If you focus on the doing part, you'll be fine. I usually do 20 reps standing as a warm-up set with no weights, mimicking the movement I will use for the seated lateral raises. Simulating the exercise gives me the correct feel to prepare for my working set form. So let's proceed to the training portion. Use some principles from the previous chapters to create your variations. I've always felt these variations are the most effective for exponential growth:

o   Variation #1:

Set #1 -- Warm Up Set for "feel" as you stand, mimicking movement (20 reps).

Set #2 -- Power Bomb

o   Variation #2:

Set #1 -- Warm Up Set for "feel" as you stand, mimicking movement (20 reps)

Set #2 -- Explosive Rep with 3 Second Contraction Hold at shoulder level, 5 Second Negative on the way down. Repeat reps until failure.

Set #3 -- Quick reps to failure with 30 rep target. If you hit failure at 14, for example, perform 16 partials at the lower part of the movement to have 30 reps.

Set #4 -- Combine #1 and #2 -- Explosive Rep with 3 Second Contraction Hold at shoulder level, 5 Second Negative on the way down. Repeat reps until failure. If you hit failure at 8 reps doing this, perform 22 partials at the lower part of the movement to have 30 reps.

Keep things simple when you come up with your variations. Overcomplicating movements to seem sophisticated is an area where a lot of lifters falter. Ironically, looking cool with unique, over-the-top workouts and routines will lead to a below-average physique.

Instead of trying to look cool, be cool with how your muscles look as a recognition of the fact. Staying focused, indirectly progressing, body and mind, and simplicity will put you in a different stratosphere than all those others. These principles require looking inward and not outward. The simpler and more efficient you get, the more time and mental energy you'll have for those power moments expressed before. One day you'll be at the gym, and someone will approach you and ask, "What do you do to get your shoulders that way"? Without even realizing it, you indirectly look fantastic now. But it won't matter to you because you strive for something greater every day.

Chest

Workout #1: Incline or Regular Bench with Dumbbell Superset Process

Workout #2: Powerbomb Machine Flyes, Cable Flyes, or Lower Chest Dips on Machine.

Front Delts

Workout #3: 3 Sets for Shoulder Press Superset with Dumbbell Front Raises

Medial Delts (Side)

Workout #4: Variation 1 for Powerbomb Method or Variation 2 for 3 Sets (not including warm-up).

Chapter 5: Mastery Approach (Triceps)

The principles we have discussed in previous chapters revolve around the mindset of being process-oriented, not event-oriented. The event is ordinarily what your ambition is. It might be losing fat, increasing muscle mass, or growing/developing one specific area. Being process-oriented will get you to the event in question. But being event oriented will constantly disrupt your process. The process is everything, and the event is fundamentally irrelevant. Creating chaos within a structure will shock your muscles consistently, while the structure serves as a means to exploit what works consistently. For example, I know that when I consume protein every 3 to 4 hours, either through food or a shake, my growth is inevitable. The process of having protein every 3-4 hours ensures the event of muscle growth. The event is uncertain when I break away from consuming protein between the window stated above.

If you get bored of the structure of your consistent workouts, you are failing at the chaos portion. You are not getting creative enough with your partials, increased hold on contractions, coming down slower on the negative, pushing up slower or faster on the positive, or other variations in your structure. The variations you are creating are becoming too predictable. Let's use the simple Incline Bench Press as an example without adding the Coffin Presses or Dumbbell Presses. After your warm-up, you have a moderate amount of weight on there. You push one rep explosively, then come down very slow for 4 seconds, extremely controlled. You try another rep explosively and come down very slow for 6 seconds. You push another rep explosively and come down for 8 seconds. You go another and come down for 10 seconds. Another, then 6 seconds. And another for 4 seconds, but you add partials at the bottom portion until failure on that last rep. Structure and chaos are working in harmony throughout that whole example. There's a pattern of the explosive rep, the two-second increments for the negative portion on your first few sets. Then, an unexpected decrease of 4 seconds on the negative, followed by a 2-second reduction for the negative part on the last few sets, then partials to ensure new muscle fiber creation. Think of the following quote when you approach a straightforward workout movement to creatively maximize it:

"I fear not the man who has practiced 10,000 kicks once, but I fear the man who has practiced one kick 10,000 times" – Bruce Lee.

This statement holds in so many ways. Notice in the example described above how the simple Incline Bench Press is only limited by your creativity. Using your imagination to gauge your muscles' response to a stimulus will determine what you filter out for future use. You will notice what your muscles respond to best with enough practice and repetition. You'll be able to detect this by the degree of pump & burn your muscles experience. Then you can keep those movements your muscles respond best to and discard those where you don't feel the desired response. Process, Mastery, plus Body & Mind Connection work in conjunction with one another to achieve this. It is your prerogative what to discard and what to keep. Have faith in your ability to have thousands of options, in one movement, with one grip.

This concept works wonders when training your Triceps after completing your Chest and Shoulders. The key here is realizing the amount of work your Triceps have undertaken thus far. During the Chest portion, your Triceps received a lot of work when pressing on the Incline and Dips. Machine Flyes give your Triceps a slight break. So planning which methods to begin with is vital to get rest strategically, without completely cooling down. When you trained shoulders right after Chest, the shoulder presses also gave your Triceps good work and power. The Lateral Machine Raises gave your Triceps a slight break once again. You're starting to see a pattern here. So now, when we move on to train Triceps after Lateral Machine Raises, they have already been exposed to a lot of work and power. They have rested enough to go for one last workout to finish them off for outstanding Tricep development. They don't need much work anymore, but they must be shocked to finish this fantastic Push routine. All you need to train them is to perform Rope Pull Downs or V Bar Pull Downs. Nothing else is required or is as effective as those two. I will describe how to approach it, so there is no doubt about the development you desire.

The structure will remain simple, and the chaos portion will also remain simple. A rule of thumb you should follow mindset-wise is this: The fresher a muscle group is, the chaos portion's intensity must match the proportion of how fresh the muscle group is. If the muscle group has already been taxed, you must keep the chaos portion and shocking principles simple. You had noticed this being the case from when we began Chest – the structure and chaos were more complex. When we moved on to shoulders, the chaos portion became more straightforward and direct, with fewer sets involved. As you move through your workout, technique becomes essential and slowly substitutes intensity.

In the beginning, intensity and chaos are paramount. As we move closer to the end, technique and focus take the lead. It would be best if you approached Triceps with an impeccable emphasis on technique and less on intensity. The rope will serve the purpose of creating separation and development on the Triceps. The V Bar will serve the purpose of power and strength. You can stick to the rope only or the V Bar only. Or you can combine the approach as well.

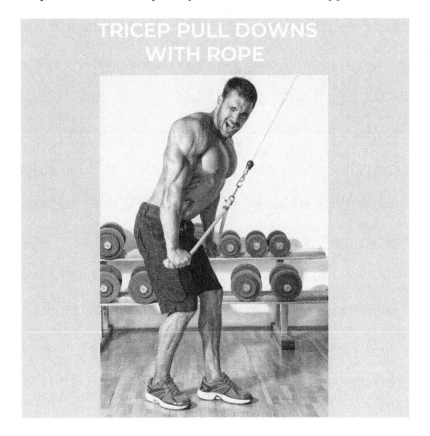

TRICEP PULL DOWNS
WITH STRAIGHT BAR

Make sure to flex your Triceps after every set significantly. A 10-second flex is ideal. You will target your Triceps with 5 sets to finish them off and finally complete. If you go the rope-only route for your 5 sets, I find this way to be the most effective:

1. 15-20 reps at a light to medium weight. The reps must be done explosively—just quick reps with no contraction or anything else. Just go! Make sure your arms don't sway, and your shoulders don't move. Completely isolate the movement. Extreme flex triceps after the set.

2. You must perform reps to failure without counting reps after increasing the weight slightly from the last set. The movement is slow and controlled. Use the Mastery Approach. Contract and flex for varying times. I find that 1-3 seconds works best. Go up slowly and control the negative for 3-5 seconds. Extreme flex the Triceps after the set.

3. Keep the weight the same as set #2. Here you will use a bit of momentum to make the pull-down motion lighter than the negative motion away from your body. All reps are done this way. So use slight momentum, cheating just a bit, to pull. Then hold a 1-second flexed contraction, then go up slowly for 5 seconds. This set is centered on the slight momentum

and negative focus. The positive movement is not the concern here. Extreme flex the Triceps after the set.

4. Increase the weight a little bit and repeat the process of set #3. Extreme flex the Triceps after the set.

5. Increase the weight once again and repeat the process of set #1. But this time, go to failure and don't count your reps! Extreme flex the Triceps for the last time.

The Rope Pull Down route is centered around a lighter to intermediate weight emphasis. In contrast, the V Bar route is centered around a medium to heavier emphasis. Notice how the rope route focuses more on contraction and the negative portion of the movement. Your rope reps should be more controlled than the V Bar route. It is not as necessary to contract as long or focus on the negative portion as much for the V Bar. The approach is more power based. The contraction is about half a second. It is there but should not take as long. The positive movement is the primary focus. The 5th set requires two drop sets. If you go the V Bar route, I find this way to be the most effective:

1. Start with an intermediate amount of weight. Push those reps without counting until failure. Extreme flex after the set is complete.

2. Increase the weight and repeat

3. Increase the weight and repeat

4. Increase the weight and repeat

5. Increase the weight and go to failure. Proceed to drop the weight by half and continue to failure. Drop weight once again and finish off to failure once again. There is no need to flex on this final set. It would be overkill, so end the set.

You can also combine the Rope Pull Down and the V Bar Pull Down for an incredible shock if you have the energy for it mentally and physically. Alternating between both works very well, but it also requires changing from the rope to the V Bar. Sometimes one or the other is not readily available at the gym. Equipment scarcity must be taken into consideration when performing Triceps. Every approach we take is efficient, and waiting for someone to finish with either the rope or the V Bar wastes time. When you acquire one, exploit it. Maybe you can buy your rope and have it in your gym bag, so you only have to worry about obtaining the V Bar. But if both are readily available for you without restriction, then you can go the following route with slight adjustments in the rope portion:

1. (Rope with rep adjustment) 10-15 reps at a light to medium weight. These reps must be done explosively—just quick reps with no contraction or anything else. Just go! Make sure your arms don't sway, and your shoulders don't move. Completely isolate the movement. Extreme flex triceps after the set.

2. (Rope with contraction adjustment) Reps to failure without counting reps after increasing the weight slightly from the last set. You don't want to contract too much since you need a reserve of output for the V-Bar in sets #4 and #5. Those sets are slow and controlled. Use the Mastery Approach. Contract and flex for 1 second. Go up slowly on the negative controlled for 3 seconds. Extreme flex the Triceps after the set.

3. (Rope) Increase the weight slightly and repeat set #2

4. (V Bar) Increase the weight to a heavy range. Perform reps to failure

5. (V Bar) Increase the weight and go to failure. Drop the weight by half and continue to failure. Drop weight once again and finish off to failure once again. There is no need to flex on this final set. It would be overkill. Just end the set.

That run-down covers the Push routine for day 1 of your 3-day split. Notice the Structure below. Pay attention to how each part we train is pushed to its maximum potential to shock with our chaos principles, and yet, also serves as a warm-up for the next upcoming part:

Day 1 Push Summary

o **Chest**

1. Incline Bench or Regular Bench Compounded with Coffin Presses (Focused Approach Process)

2. Power Bomb for Machine Flyes, Cable Flyes, or Machine Dips

o **Shoulders (Anterior Head)**

3. Shoulder Press with Dumbbell Raises (3 sets)

o **Shoulders (Middle Head)**

4. Lateral Machine Raises (3 sets)

o **Triceps**

5. Rope Pull Downs/ V Bar Pull Downs (5 sets)

As I stated in Chapter 1, the Chest portion can begin with any three options. You can start at Machine Dips with an emphasis on your Lower Chest by leaning forward, making sure not to involve your Triceps. Then you can move on to Machine Flyes. Finally, you can finish Chest off with Incline Bench Compounded with Coffin Presses. Any combination of those three will work using the chaos principles. They are interchangeable. The Shoulders and Tricep portions are not interchangeable. Keep them as structured above. When you're starting to feel weaker or sensing a lack of density, you can shift focus to a more focused power approach for Chest, then go The Power Bomb route when you target the Shoulders and Triceps to get a quick intensity workout. Balance your structure as you see fit. There is such thing as too much intensity and too much power. You must decide when to shift focus – an essential step in mastery.

Side Note: Please rate and review this book if you bought it on Amazon. It helps tremendously. Thank you very much.

Chapter 6: Technician Approach (Back)

Your philosophy regarding injury will determine how far you progress and transcend the limitations of your physique. This is not to say that being tough and pushing through injuries is wise, but training has a consistency component that can't be overlooked. Consistency and frequency are essential in the pursuit of your desired transformation. There's a downside to such consistency and frequency, though. Injuries happen with the same consistency and frequency, as well. The most detrimental injuries are shoulder, knee, back, wrist, and elbow. They are some of the most stubborn injuries. They happen consistently, one right after the other. It seems like when one part heals, another part gets injured. So if you're ever wholly injury-free, please cherish those divine weeks.

There is an approach you can take to continue to make progress even through the injury. This approach will take you from being an average lifter to something beyond that. The approach you can't forget when dealing with an injury is The Technician Approach. If you ever get injured, please refer to this Chapter for a refresher. Some individuals have a lot of drive but hardly focus on technique. They train hard, and they go hard. They never quit and never settle. Or so their T-Shirts say. You see that person often. They lack form and technique, but damn, they go for it.

Then some are all about form and Hypertrophy. They watch some guys or gals on YouTube, take their clickbait advice as gospel, and follow it to the "T," yet they look the same year after year. So the avid viewer who follows said individual goes to the gym with a unique mindset focused only on PR (personal record) and form. They hit PRs here and there and get excited. They turn into an event-oriented, not process-oriented individual. Even with the PR and impeccable form, there's no progress. Please don't confuse form with technique. Form is doing the movement correctly, and technique is manipulating the movement to involve or not involve other parts or even joints-- it's a transcendence of form.

Let's say you injure your elbow performing a Tricep or Bicep movement. You come to the gym and want to hit your Lats, but your elbow limits you. At this point, form and PRs do nothing to assist in the form of progress. The elbow hurts as you extend it. And the pain is not mild. It hurts! So tell me, can you figure out an angle or a movement to hit your Lats without your elbow hurting? Figuring out the solution to such a question is the path to being a Technician. There needs to be an assured stubbornness to propel you forward because you know there's always a way. You're sure of it, and you figure it out. The natural predisposition for most people is to refrain from using the elbow completely. This incorrect disposition will tax weeks of progress away from you, which is unacceptable in my book. When you figure out how to get around the pain, it builds confidence in you. It would be best to get around the pain, not push through it. There is a difference.

To get around the pain, you must conceive new pain-free movements. Such unique exercises must work the muscle you want to target to the same degree it did before. We can take the situation one step further and use the new pain-free movement/technique to grow the muscle, not just maintain it. The indirect future benefit has this unique technique in your back pocket to use in case a similar injury happens again. Next time if you injure that part again, it's not a big deal. The situation will be slightly annoying. Remember that a tiny bit of progress is way better than regression. Progress compounds itself along with your knowledge and confidence. So use The Technician Approach for injuries when they arise because a breakthrough might be around the corner that could be a game-changer for you.

My experience with The Technician Approach led me to build a Back I never thought possible. And I owe it all to a terrible elbow injury. I could not curl or perform my usual horizontal close grip back rows. I'm sure you've had this type of injury before where all hope is sucked out of you. That's exactly how I felt. At the time, I wasn't sure why I was so enamored with my back routine. It had been years since I had made any progress. But there I was, continuing to stick to a routine out of habit and comfort. You might be in the same boat as we speak, clinging to a routine because you're comfortable with it. Or maybe you do it out of habit. But, even if you enjoy your routine, you have to make progress. I don't just mean making the type of progress where you break personal records. I mean pursuing actual progress, growing in such a way that you pass an obvious visual test. The elbow injury was the best thing that ever happened to me.

One day I was researching new methods to apply in my current circumstances. Most of the things I found were, "Lay off of it until it heals completely." Excellent advice. But not an option for me because it goes against my nature. Relentlessly, my belief stays firm that there is always a way. So I shifted away from useless advice and started to watch interviews of the greats – the Golden Era bodybuilders. Those old-school-obsessed individuals. Dorian Yates and Arnold Schwarzenegger interviews were some that I found. Halfway through watching one of Arnold's interviews, he began to talk about the beauty of bodybuilding and his fascination with different training styles differing from his own. He went on about how he admired specific individuals who trained differently than he did. Arnold begins to talk about a particular individual he once knew with an incredible back. According to him, it was one of the best Backs he's ever seen. The guy he talked about was some unknown lifter who never made it big. This individual apparently only trained Back vertically, never horizontally.

When Back day rolled around again, the vertical way of training was on my mind. So I decided to try it out for at least two weeks, hoping there was something to it. Saying the vertical way of training my Back changed everything for me is an understatement. Those two weeks turned into months, and those months have turned into years. The vertical back strategy is an incredible one. I'll shortly explain why this vertical-focused training has so many benefits. But first, let's cover a few things. How many people, men or women, do you often see with an incredible back that makes you think – "Wow!"? If I could guess, you probably think the occurrence is rare. It is infrequent. Here's another question. How often do you see people performing, with perfect form, Horizontal Back Rows on the cable machine or the Overhead Wide Grip Pull Downs on the cable machine? Most likely every day without fail. Do you see the disconnect here? Why do so many people have seemingly perfect form when executing those two popular workouts, but their backs are way below average? Here are three reasons why:

1. **Your Back is mighty:** For your Back to grow, the "usual" requirement is training it at every angle possible, at a very heavy weight and high rep.

2. **Your biceps:** Your biceps will always give out before your Back. Even with impeccable form, most people pull with their biceps excessively when training back without realizing it. As a result, the Back never truly activates, no matter how perfect the

form. Sometimes the biceps are too strong and overtake the movement.

3. **Size maintenance problem:** The more muscle you develop on your back, the more calories and protein you need to maintain and grow. You might only grow in low visual impact areas, which makes it seem like your Back is underdeveloped.

Whenever you encounter problems in your training, it requires solving each problem precisely. What I describe are guidelines to assist you in your training approach. You don't have to do it the way I describe strictly. As long as you understand the concept and adapt it accordingly, you become more experienced. If you can find a better way, please go for it. Efficiency and finding better ways is what this book is about. Here is how I solved the issues above:

o **Solving for #1:** Discard the impulse of training at every angle. Instead, focus on targeting two main angles using chaos principles discussed in previous chapters. For the first angle, target the Lat spread doing Wide Grip Overhead Lat Pull Down on a cable machine or something comparable. For the second angle, target the V Taper. The muscle that ties down to your lower Back. Reverse grip overhead pull-downs where the bar hits the middle of your chest while driving with elbows near your waist perfectly target the V Taper. Research workouts on targeting V Taper for additional exercises. There are many out there.

o **Solving for #2:** Pre-exhaust your Lats with Straight Arm Pull Downs using the short, straight bar. I don't mean a few sets to get a workout in. Destroy your Back doing these using chaos principles. Then you can proceed to Lat Spread focus or V Taper focus. Your Back will activate much better, and any unwanted help from the biceps becomes an asset at this point.

o **Solving for #3:** You want to choose your deficiencies strategically. The hack is having a visually perfect Back without it being the case. Your Back will look as if it is completely developed. Achieving this will guarantee other parts grow proportionally. With less unnecessary mass on your back, your nutrition resources will be allotted to growing other areas, such as your shoulders, chest, and arms.

Now that we've solved for those three issues, fittingly applying the solutions to create a streamlined program becomes much more manageable. Contrary to popular belief, there is no reason to invest most of our time training Back. Most people spend over an hour training Back with minimal results. I will show you how to do it quicker for maximum effect without the deficiencies associated with prolonged exercise. About 30 minutes will suffice, which gives you time to train rear delts, biceps, and traps – in that order. After completing **The Straight Arm Pull Overs to Pre-Exhaust** below, you want to choose between **Wide Grip Lat Pull Downs** or **Underhand Lat Pull Downs**. Don't perform both. There's a specific reason for that I will later explain. For now, choose where you are weakest and require more growth/ development.

LAT PULL DOWNS

UNDERHAND LAT PULL DOWNS

So let's begin with the Back portion of your training. Remember, what I show you below is just an example. Use your chaos principles to adjust the times and tempos, or mix and match as you wish. You are advanced enough by now to be thinking like a technician. Nothing is set in stone, and what's below is only my preference. The structure for every set will look something like this:

○ **Straight Arm Pullovers to Pre-Exhaust Back Before Pulling Movements (2 warm-up sets; 4 working sets):**

1. Warm up with a weight light enough to efficiently perform 20 reps and feel a slight burn. Nowhere near failure

2. Another warm-up set with the same weight and the same concept

3. Increase the weight slightly. Pull explosively, hold for 1 second, then release slowly for 5 seconds. Do this until failure. Flex your Back extremely for 5 seconds after the set is done.

4. Increase the weight to a moderate amount now. Use momentum when you pull to make the weight lighter, then release slowly for 5 seconds. This whole set is based on the pulling motion being lighter than the release. Do this to failure. Flex again for 5 seconds after the set is done.

5. Repeat #4

6. Increase the weight to a heavy range. Perform the reps with power and explosiveness with no regard for the release. Just get the reps done. Once you hit failure, quickly drop the weight by half and perform reps to failure again. Once that is done, quickly drop the weight by half once again and go to failure. Flex your Back for a final time once this last set is done.

o **Wide Grip Lat Pull Down (4 Sets for Power)**

1. The weight should be at a moderate level. Once again, use momentum when you pull to make the weight lighter. Hold and contract for 1 second, then release slowly for 5

seconds. It would be best if you focused on stretching those Lats on that negative release. This whole set is based on the pulling motion being lighter than the release. Do this to failure.

2. Increase the weight slightly and repeat #1.

3. Increase the weight to a heavy range. Then, knock out reps until failure without worrying about anything else.

4. Increase the weight to a heavier amount now. Once you hit failure, quickly drop the weight by half and perform reps to failure again. Once that is done, quickly drop the weight by half once again and go to failure.

o   **Underhand Lat Pull Down (4 Sets; Light to Moderate weight; More controlled)**

1. The weight should be at a light level. Pull regularly, hold a 3-second contraction at the bottom, and release slowly for 3 seconds. Extreme flex your Back for 5 seconds after the set is done.

2. Increase the weight slightly and repeat #1.

3. At a moderate weight, use momentum when you pull to make the weight lighter. Hold and contract for 1 second, then release slowly for 5 seconds. It would help if you focused on stretching those Lats on that negative release. This whole set is based on the pulling motion being lighter than the release. Do this to failure. Extreme Flex your Back for 5 seconds

4. Repeat #3. Once you hit failure, drop the weight by half quickly. Hit failure again and drop the weight once again by half. Go to failure again.

Those vertical angles revealed above will give your Back a visual appearance as if you perform every angle. Your upper will look wide from the back view and the front and will also tie up nicely to your waist. From the side view, your Back will look thick due to your Tricep pushing up against your wide Lats. Inadvertently, your Triceps will also look bigger from that side view due to how wide your Lats are as they push against them. So following your Push routine properly for the Triceps portion has indirect benefits on the overall visual -- creating that beautiful and powerful aesthetic only a few have. With this knowledge and wisdom, you will undoubtedly be a part of those few.

Chapter 7: Isolation Approach (Rear Delts)

How can a muscle needing just a few sets be one of the most challenging to develop properly? The posterior head of the shoulder, or Rear Delt as is commonly known, is such a muscle. Unfortunately, this underrated part is seldom a lifter's primary focus. You can train them in less than 10 minutes, but it can take years to get the right feel to activate growth. As a result, rear delts are either trained at the end of a workout or avoided altogether. After this Chapter, that will no longer be the case for you. They will become priority number two after your Lats are meticulously targeted on those critical angles. Sexy muscles such as the Biceps and Chest get all the attention, and rightfully so. The rear delts, however, will determine at what point those sexy muscles plateau, plus a few others. When you bench, they can assist in having the weight feel lighter than it is. Such a feeling of lightness is also the case when performing any other stabilizing movement. The more lightweight feel of the weight will increase your confidence on the lift and push of the exercise—a sort of psychological benefit per se. Once rear delts are adequately developed, your arms and shoulders will manifest a superior quality rarely seen.

Before any of what I just mentioned becomes your powerful default, you need to start thinking in terms of isolation to achieve that higher level. This beneficial thought process is what I used to solve the rear delt development issue for myself. And you can use it too, effectively. Once I teach you this thought process, you can use it at your discretion when attempting other workouts where stubborn muscles are prevalent. The main issue with low-quality rear delts is the lack of effective training when tackled. Suppose they are even tackled at all. A secondary issue revolves around the lack of isolation in the target area because the focus is a compound movement. The trick is to isolate as much as possible using proper grip position on the Fly Machine, positioned for Rear Delts instead of the Chest. The arm position works best on that close, over-hand grip, where your thumbs touch each other. Your arm position must be aligned perfectly with your Rear Delts, not higher, and not lower. Knowing this is the first step. There's a second step that involves the other grip where palms are facing one another. The starting position looks similar to the end position of a Chest Fly when you contract. Keep these two hand positions in mind as I describe how to use The Isolation Approach.

Whether you're on the Fly Machine or bent over with your torso parallel to the ground using dumbbells to perform Rear Delt Flyes, the isolation movement is the overhand grip with thumbs right next to each other. If you can do 10lb dumbbells to failure for 12 reps, using the grip I just described, and 12 reps to failure using palms facing each other type grip with 20lb dumbbells, then that means the first grip gives you an extremely high level of isolation compared to the second. Being able to push more weight is not always a good thing. When you align your arm movement perfectly using the palms facing each other grip, a heavier weight will be necessary to reach failure. The higher weight capability should tell you there's a lack of isolation on Rear Delts, and Traps/Lats might be getting involved.

You won't need as much weight using the overhand grip. To simplify things, follow these guidelines:

1. Make overhand grip positive movement intensive since it is isolated. Push for high reps without worrying too much about

the negative or holding a contraction at the end of the rep— Flex Rear Delts after each set.

2. Make palms facing each other grip negative intensive. The Lats will be involved in the positive movement, but it doesn't matter because your focus will be the slower negative at the higher weight level. Flex Rear Delts after each set.

3. Combine #1 and #2. Go to failure on the overhand grip. Switch to palms facing each other grip, and continue the set. Flex Rear Delts after each set.

4. Combine #1 and #2. Go heavy on the first set with palms facing each other to failure, drop weight by half quickly, and go to failure again. Next set, switch to an overhand grip and repeat the same process.

You only need about three sets. After completing this book's Back portion, make sure you jump straight into Rear Delts, following the guidelines above. More than three sets will persistently lead you into the "wasted set" realm most people find themselves in. To avoid such a downfall, you must ask yourself if the set you're about to do is even necessary. There is a vast difference between pushing yourself beyond your limits and extending an inefficient workout, so you feel accomplished. Make sure to create your structure for those three sets. And don't forget to apply those chaos principles, as well. Get creative and make it your own. Using the overhand grip, isolate those Rear Delts as much as you can. And make sure to use the palms facing each other grip to continue the set when the Isolated target reaches failure.

Back

Workout #1: Pre-Exhaust with 4 Sets of Isolated Straight Arm Lat Pullovers

Workout #2: 4 Sets of Wide Grip Lat Pull Downs for Power

Workout #3: 4 Sets of Underhand Lat Pull Downs Light to Moderate use Ch.6 example.

Rear Delts

Workout #4: 3 Sets on Fly Machine adjusted for Rear Delts

Chapter 8: Biceps, Traps, and Forearms

Apart from Chest and Shoulders, one of the most coveted muscles is Biceps. My hope for this Chapter is to increase your intimate knowledge of them. Your understanding will be so rich that nothing will stop you from building them in the shape or form you want. Most of the information I will provide can't be found anywhere else. The diamond in the rough type of expertise champions keep to themselves. So while everyone else is doing the same thing, from the same sources, getting the same results, you will have something unique they can't match. You may have heard of the proper form for Biceps and applied it accordingly in the past, with subpar results. But what you'll soon read goes beyond proper form. You will be an artist, and your Biceps will be your canvas. You'll become adept at achieving any size, shape, or aesthetic definition.

The right way of targeting a muscle can sometimes be subjective. Lifting, I believe, is more art than science. There's a particular flow and skill behind every movement and the focus that goes along with it. There's a style and beauty to it. Science and structure only complement art, but they cannot replace it. The science aspect has taken over processes for weightlifting and body composition transformation.

In contrast, artful psychology is being left out of it altogether. Such neglect is a huge mistake. Once I teach you the logic behind every movement, it's on you to turn your piece of clay into a work of art. Next, I'll point out how much paint to use on your brush on which part of the canvas. Too much color without a fine brush stroke will make your painting unappealing. Think of your chest, shoulders, and arms the same way—the right amount of, with the right intent, in the right spot.

I learned most of this information in small fragments through the years. I finally have the whole picture with each piece of information, and my passion for sharing this with you is unmatched. Those fragments are similar to parts of a puzzle. Some of you might have only a few pieces, and others might have incorrect ones. Either truth would give you the wrong picture. Below I will provide you with the WHOLE adding a few common sense fundamentals. If you follow these Ten Fundamentals, your Biceps will transform. They are explained below by priority. So let's get to it.

10 Bicep Fundamentals:

1) Target the whole Bicep by aligning your wrist perfectly with it. This will allow your Bicep to grow evenly. Imagine an invisible line from the center of your Bicep going to the middle of your wrist. Using the EZ bar to curl with hands at an angle facing each other breaks this rule.

2) It would be best to have constant tension at the movement's top and bottom. Contract and squeeze at the top. Then on the way down, when the Bicep reaches its lowest point, make sure it doesn't get any rest. Keep tension at the bottom as well. The Bicep must have constant tension. Individual bicep curls alternating between one arm and the other break this rule. One of them hangs on the side while the other one is just hanging there. Stop doing those alternating curls. If you use dumbbells, make sure to curl with both arms simultaneously. Curling with both hands is also more efficient. It takes less than half the time compared to doing single-arm dumbbell bicep curls.

3) The positive full range must have complete isolation. Positive motion is where 60% of your progress will come from. Most people make the mistake of curling their forearms (moving their wrists) slightly at the beginning and middle of the movement. Even slight wrist movements should be avoided. **So, try keeping your wrist straight throughout the curl**. You'll feel a massive difference on how your bicep feels – better burn and pump. Think of your forearm as an extension of the arm only. It should

be straight and fixed from the beginning of the action until the end. Common sense dictates the power your forearm has. Just think about it—forearms are used for everything. When you curl, if you move your forearm even slightly, those are pounds removed from the tension that should have gone to the Biceps. Isolate the Bicep by keeping the forearms completely stiff and straight.

4) The entire negative range will be about 40% of your progress. After contraction, the slower you come down, the more of a percentage you target. You can use the concept of the positive movement being lighter than the negative portion of the force from Chapter 1 to create new muscle fibers if the weight is not heavy enough to risk injury, usually 50%-60% of your one rep max. You can cheat just a bit on the way up and come down very slow. Focus the whole set and every rep doing that. The lighter positive and heavier negative will destroy that 40% and create new muscle fibers—just a small hack for you to be aware of.

5) The positive half range isolates even further. Beginning your curls from the half range, with forearms parallel to the ground,

eliminate the forearm involvement problem. The downside is the lack of full range and stretch on the Bicep at the lower portion. To maximize the effect of this principle, perform The Power Bomb Method with half-range curls using the short bar on the cable machine. It is safe, quick, and efficient. The Power Bomb at the half range will also create new fibers, increase your vascularity, and deplete glycogen rapidly. Remember that depleting glycogen gives the same effect as being on a low-carb diet.

6) Flex and contract your Biceps after every set. Flexing and contracting will maintain a fantastic peak. Make sure to squeeze to an extreme for at least 10 seconds. Remember Arnold using this strategy after every muscle set to provide additional size and definition.

7) The lower part of the Bicep is also essential. It gives it that amazing round look as it ties to the forearm. It has an aesthetic beauty to it that transcends size. To achieve this, you must focus on the full range and keep the tension at the bottom as much as

possible. A neat hack is doing 20 partials concentrated on the bottom quarter of the Bicep.

8) It would be best to achieve vascularity, tightness, and separation stemming from shoulder to forearm. Achieve this by doing high rep sets. Rep range should be about 20-30 reps, where failure lands somewhere between. The Power Bomb full range also works.

9) Achieve the thickness of it. Heavy hammer curls or The Power Bomb using the rope in a hammer fashion on the cable machine

10) Prioritize heavyweight for Biceps. But make sure to finish them off with The Power Bomb or 1 set of high rep 20-30 rep range. I will give you variations at the end of the Chapter, so you know exactly how and when to go heavy and high rep.

Yes, I know. Those are a lot of fundamentals. Training the seemingly simple Biceps is a complex process. Now you see why most people never achieve the type of Bicep development they long for. Attempting so would require some semblance of wisdom regarding the fundaments stated. Articulating this knowledge is not an easy task. Professionals with a high level of expertise have difficulty explaining such a process. They might know how to train the Biceps, but articulating such complexities doesn't come easy. Now that you have this information, you can exercise your biceps to suit your needs. As with previous chapters, I will present two variations to facilitate your journey through the process. Developing your own using this book's principles, methods, and approaches is vital.

TRAIN BOTH BICEPS WHEN USING DUMBBELLS

The two variations are as follows:

➤ Size and Strength (Follow Principles)

Set #1: Light Warmup. Do a 10-rep light warmup using 5lb-15lb dumbbells. Even if you're powerful, stick to that range.

- Proceed with two "feel" sets. The feel sets facilitate the journey to those Power sets. We covered this concept in Chapter 1. The purpose of these sets is not to go to failure. The objective is to prepare. Adjust your weight according to your strength level. Use my concept as a guide. My feel sets look something like this:

Set # 2: Barbell Only (45 lbs) for 10 reps when my failure is 20.

Set #3: Barbell + 10's (65 lbs) for 7 reps when my failure is 18.

- These following be your Power Sets. Use The Focused Approach. The goal is to get as near your 1 Rep Max as possible. Shoot for your 3 Rep Max to start. Then the weight will be lowered to maintain a heavy failure level. Your muscles only understand heavy, not necessarily a specific weight number. You will reduce the weight slightly to trick your muscles into thinking it is the same resistance as before:

Set #4: Barbell + 35's (115 lbs) for 3 rep failure

Set #5: Barbell + 45's (135 lbs) for 1-2 rep failure

Set #6: Barbell + 35's (115 lbs) for 1 rep failure

Set #7: Barbell + 25's (95 lbs) for as many reps possible

- Due to the low intensity of these strength and size-centric sets, I prefer a quick, high-intensity, high rep set. Therefore, I go for an all-out attack.

Final Bonus Set: The Power Bomb Method on the cable machine is what I use. Do it with a straight bar or rope. You can also grab some light weight and do as many reps as possible. 30+ reps is what you should shoot for.

POWER BOMB WITH ROPE FOR BICEPS

➤ Tightness, Definition, Vascularity, & Separation

Set #1: Warmup. Do a 10 rep light warmup using 5lb-15lb dumbbells. Even if you're really strong, stick to that range.

- These following sets are alternating in pairs. The total is 6 sets. You will perform regular curls using dumbbells for each hand. For me the weights are 15lb dumbbells, 20lb, and 25lb. Alternate to Hammer curls using the same weight. You will increase the weight and repeat the process. Rest maximum one minute after every set.

Set #2: 15lb Regular for 20-30 reps, where failure lands in between.

Set #3: 15lb Hammer for 20-30 reps, where failure lands in between

Set #4: 20lb Regular for 20-30 reps

Set # 5: 20lb Hammer for 20-30 reps

Set #6: 25lb Regular for 12-20 reps

Set #7: 25lb Hammer for 12-20 reps

Even if you don't come up with your own variations, the two I just provided will build your Biceps above and beyond what most people have. Those two variations are my favorite. One thing that may assist you is thinking of your biceps in terms of parts. Think of the whole, the top, and the bottom. Make sure to always keep tension through the whole movement, from top to bottom. The Bicep should get zero rest throughout. Focus on power with complete control, then high rep or Power Bomb to finish them off and destroy. You have the tools now to get those fantastic Biceps you've always wanted.

Traps and Forearms: What makes the streamlined approach to training so great is the indirect benefit of each training day. As you transition from each workout to the next, muscles that are next in the process have either been warmed up or slightly worked -- reducing the lag time between sets and avoiding wasted sets with no benefit. When you train your back, your biceps warm up, your rear delts get slight work, and your traps get slight work. When you proceed to rear delts, your biceps will get a bit more work, and your traps will also get a bit more work. Your forearms get a contraction/static effect when you proceed to biceps. The streamlined process is why spending 20-30 minutes training traps and forearms after all those workouts will cause overtraining and wasted sets with no benefit.

Target a total of 5 sets for both lasting 10 minutes. Always do traps first. It could be 3 sets for traps and 2 sets for forearms. If you do a Powerbomb set for traps and 2 sets for forearms, then you should complete both in 5 minutes. This is more efficient, but make sure to switch it up. Or the inverse. These are the principles to maximize your gains for those two body parts at the end of your workout:

- Powerbomb for Traps on cable machine.

- Four Ranges of Failure can be used for both Traps & Forearms. An example is in the Calves Chapter (Chapter 13). You can also use Four Ranges of Failure for Quads on the Pre-Exhaust portion, For Bicep Curls, and Tricep Pulldowns.

- Traps and Forearms respond exceptionally well to contraction—contract for 1 second minimum at the top of every rep. And flex/contract after every set as well for 10 seconds.

Day 2 Pull Summary

Back

Workout #1: Pre-Exhaust with 4 Sets of Isolated Straight Arm Lat Pullovers

Workout #2: 4 Sets of Wide Grip Lat Pull Downs for Power

Workout #3: 4 Sets of Underhand Lat Pull Downs Light to Moderate use Ch.6 example.

Rear Delts

Workout #4: 3 Sets on Fly Machine adjusted for Rear Delts.

Biceps

Workout #5: Size and Strength Process or Tightness, Definition, Vascularity, & Separation Process. Choose 1.

Traps and Forearms

Workout #6: 3 sets for Traps and 2 Sets for Forearms. Or 3 Sets for Forearms and 2 sets for Traps.

Chapter 9: Frequency, Periodization, and Split

In this Chapter, I will cover what your training split will look like. We have covered a variety of training methods, and it is time to bring it all together. The usual split individuals approach is called The Bro Split. This split is a 1x frequency per week training pattern. It consists of Chest on Day 1, Back on Day 2, Legs on Day 3, Shoulders on Day 4, and Arms on day 5. Then rest on the weekend. There are various opinions out there regarding a split setup. You would think an ideal split exists somewhere out there. Unfortunately, personal preference and bias usually take hold of such conversations. The bright side is there is a consensus regarding the benefit of frequency. You will grow more the more frequent your workouts are. One caveat to this theory is that recovery will not allow excessive frequency.

Enhanced individuals (a euphemism for people on steroids) respond best to a 3x and higher frequency. They can easily do Upper Body on Day 1, Lower Body on Day 2, Upper on Day 3, Lower on Day 4, Upper on Day 5, and Lower on Day 6. Then they rest on the 7th Day. Roided people recover quicker than most, so they can exploit frequency, hence the excessive growth. Even a 4x- 6x frequency per week of whole body workouts would not cause them to skip a beat. We are natural lifters, so we must find the ideal frequency to grow. I am confident I have found the perfect solution to such a problem. The 2x frequency is suitable for a natural lifter. In the next Chapter, I will give you a step-by-step way to supplement to make sure you recover and grow to an amateur competition-level physique.

You will have the ideal recovery for your 2x Frequency training. Our split will consist of Day 1 Push (Chapters 1- 5), Day 2 Pull (Chapters 6-8), and Day 3 Legs. Then a rest day on the 4th Day. Then you begin the cycle on the 5th Day, beginning with Push again, Pull on the 6th, then Legs on the 7th. Giving you a perfect 2x frequency routine. It will look something like this:

1) Chest, Shoulders (Front and Middle), Triceps

2) Back, Rear Delts, Biceps, Traps

3) Legs & Core

4) Rest

5) Chest, Shoulders (Front and Middle), Triceps

6) Back, Rear Delts, Biceps, Traps

7) Legs and Core

8) Rest

A benefit from this split is the periodization of your workout days. For example, you may begin Push on a Monday when everyone trains chest. But next week, on day 8th, you'll start Push on a Tuesday.

- Monday (Push)

- Tuesday (Pull)

- Wednesday (Legs)

- Thursday (Rest)

- Friday (Push)

- Saturday (Pull)

- Sunday (Legs)

- Monday (Rest)

- Tuesday (Periodized Push)

The precise rhythm for muscle growth consists of Frequency and Periodization to disrupt adaptation as a means to confuse when your muscles get used to the pattern. For example, the pattern of the split periodizes the days of the week. But there's also a way to periodize your split by training an extra day before your rest day. It resets your split to a new pattern. The process looks something like this:

Original Pattern:

1) Push

2) Pull

3) Legs

4) Rest

Additional Training Day to Periodize Split:

1) Push

2) Pull

3) Legs

4) Push

5) Rest

Periodized Split

1) Pull

2) Legs

3) Push

4) Rest.

With the periodized split, our pattern begins with Pull instead of Push. We added an extra training day to disrupt adaptation, provide Chaos, and maintain the same Structure. The core pattern remains. Just make sure to take it easy on that extra training day. You don't want to train as intensely as your previous three training days because fatigue might set in. You should never be at the gym longer than two hours. Ninety minutes is the ideal time. If you're taking longer, then that means you are not being efficient. Such precise efficiency takes time, so don't get discouraged. Practice makes perfect. To finish this Chapter up, let's tie everything nice and neat with what you should target using your new split:

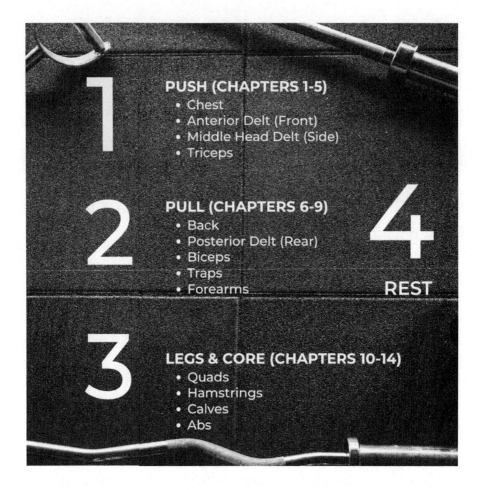

You may also decide to stick to the traditional split. It's the most common split. It's also the one most of us start with. The traditional split is:

Day 1: Chest (Chapters 1&2 for Upper Body)

Day 2: Back (Chapter 6 for Upper Body)

Day 3: Shoulders (Chapters 3, 4, & 7 for Upper Body)

Day 4: Legs

Day 5: Arms (Chapters 5 & 8 for Upper Body)

Day 6 & 7: Rest Days

That 5 day split with 2 rest days works well if you're a beginner. But not much growth happens a couple of years after. That split is a great way to maintain decent muscularity and size. I recommend you eventually transition into the Push, Pull, Legs streamlined version this book is based on. That will ensure lifelong growth and shock your muscles into growth.

Chapter 10: Pre-Exhaust Principle (Quads)

Breaking the genetic barrier in pursuing higher-level legs will be achievable with this book. You don't have to wrap your knees up like a mummy, carry a massive gym bag like you're going camping, or perform excruciating squats at dangerous levels. The methods in this book are efficient and effective. There are no wasted sets and no wasted reps. Gone are those days when people skipped leg days and only focused on their upper body. Legs have become a status symbol for higher-level achievement regarding lifting. Most people who try my books or seek coaching come to me as a last resort. I always wondered why that was. Their drive and knowledge base was there. But misconceptions, lack of efficiency, and genetics held them back.

The process of this book and training methods solve all those problems. I aim to guide your journey in achieving superior results than those with superior genetics, with a fraction of the effort. We need to be more strategic and efficient to accomplish such a task.

Arnold Schwarzenegger, the king of bodybuilding, had a genetic problem. Building high-quality calves was always an issue for him. He also had an additional problem – he was too tall to perform a proper squat. Shorter bodybuilders had an easier time achieving a full-range squat with more weight and less risk. Arnold would have to lean forward excessively, putting his lower back at risk every time. While every bodybuilder around him could squat with ease, he would struggle to be as effective. His legs were his weak point. What would you do in his situation? Most people would say the hell with it, complain about genetics, and resent those around them who put in the work to overcome those shortcomings. Not him! A problem standing in his way of being a champion needed to be solved. Arnold solved his leg problem by pre-exhausting his quads by performing extensions before moving to a compound movement such as squats.

It sounds simple enough, but the execution is not. Some intricacies need your attention. The exercise is a small fraction of what you need to build outstanding legs. Once you finish this chapter, you will have the tools to construct superior legs than those who primarily squat while reducing risk and injury significantly. Once you master pre-exhausting your quads properly and growth is consistent, your legs will become your favorite training day. The whole workout routine eventually needs to be completed in 90 minutes. To begin, it's ok to surpass the 2 hour mark since you're initially learning the concepts. Once you master the concepts, focus on becoming extremely efficient to shorten training time. Your ultimate leg training is completed in four phases.

MAX SIZE & DEFINITION IN 4 PHASES

PHASE #1	PHASE #2
Exercise #1: Extensions to Pre-Exhaust: • 2 Warm Up Sets • *4 effective sets where you focus on contraction failure, negative failure, positive failure, drop sets, and partials strategically at the perfect time.*	*Exercise #2: Power for Bigger Leg Size, Density, and Strength Adaptation* • 5 Sets Total. You increase the weight evenly until you get to the heaviest possible weight safely.
PHASE #3	**PHASE #4**
Exercise #3: Hamstring Tempo Training • 2 Warm Up Sets • 5 Working Sets • Lower back tightness or injury will be a thing of the past once you master this hamstring process. Extreme focus is key.	*Exercise #4: Calves* • 5 Total Sets while using the levels of failure learned in the extension part. And apply the new principle of 4 ranges of failure as well that will activate growth by activating fibers that are commonly neglected. .

QUAD LEG EXTENSIONS

Use to Pre-Exhaust

Before we begin the muscle-building process, we need to stretch and warm up. Stretching first and then warming up second is too inefficient. Instead, get into the habit of stretching as you do your warm-up sets. Stretch your quads, pelvis, hips, and hamstrings, then perform one warm-up set. Next, stretch once again, then do your second warm-up set. Stretching as you warm up will save you 10 minutes of gym time. Efficiency is vital in all we do. Stretching and warming up will make the weight feel much lighter. Five to 10-second stretches will suffice while you do your warm-up sets. If you stretch longer than 10 seconds, you might fatigue the muscle prematurely. Keep that in mind so you don't over stretch.

I like to perform two warm-up sets while I stretch. First, I stretch my quads, hamstrings, hips, and pelvis. Then I perform my first warm-up set. I repeat my stretch pattern and then perform my second warm-up set. Fifteen reps for each warm-up set is ideal with very light weight or resistance. You probably went too heavy if you feel a slight burn on those two warm-up sets. If you felt a slight burn during those 15 reps, you added too much weight or resistance. Adjust to a lower weight so you can efficiently perform 15 reps in each warm-up set effortlessly. Put the pin or move the tab from 30 to 60 resistance. That's an ideal range for your warm-up sets. Pick one level of resistance and accomplish both warm-up sets with that choice. If you decide to go with 40, then stick with 40. If you felt that was too light, go with 50 in your next training session. Or if it was too heavy, then go with 30 next time. Do not overthink it. A two-minute rest between those warm-up sets is ideal. Your warm-up sets should look something like this:

1. Stretch then 15 reps at 40 resistance
2. Stretch then 15 reps at 40 resistance

Once you feel warmed up, loose, and ready to go, you want to double the weight to begin your 1st working set. After the Upper Body portion, you should be familiar with the concept of a "feel set ." It sets the tone for the following higher-level sets. Of course, there's always an inconsistency regarding the first feel set. Some days it feels lighter, and some days it might feel a little heavier. This inconsistency happens because maybe you could have slept better or eaten better. Or perhaps your energy levels are lower for this particular day. Or the opposite is likely true, and today you feel strong and vigorous. Who knows? That first feel set will let you know how aggressively you should increase the weight on your following sets. Or if you should wisely ease off.

During this set, your primary focus will be on contraction. At the top of the movement, contract for 1 second, then come down at whatever tempo you desire. Keep tension through every rep. Most individuals make the mistake of losing tension and giving the muscle trained some ineffective rest. Avoid that type of useless rest if at all possible. Resting the muscle happens when the plates touch where the pin goes or tabs are. When that happens, the muscle stops working, giving them a little rest while you perform reps. DO NOT LET THE PLATES TOUCH. Keeping tension in such a manner is a good rule of thumb for any muscle you train. Always keep stress and keep the muscle at work. Your training will be leaps and bounds more efficient, keeping constant tension in mind.

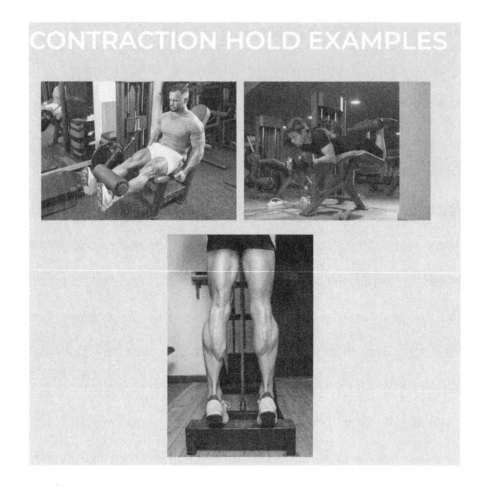

Throughout the whole process, ensure that you don't count your reps. Counting should not take over any aspect of your focus. Instead, focus on the contraction and keeping tension. When you start to feel that painful burn, continue with 3-5 more reps beyond that. Those 3-5 reps are your failure point. Once you finish your set, stand up, flex, and contract your quads for 10 seconds. Make a habit of it. That flexing habit will give you additional separation and increase your quad size. Contracting/flexing after every set is an underrated method seldom used. Seize the opportunity.

How you feel during your first set will determine the range and effort of your second set. There will be times when your energy levels are lower, or you feel weaker. During such instances, increase the weight by one or two levels. So, if you have the pin at 80lbs, increase it to 90 or 100. You can bump it up by 3 to 4 levels if you feel strong and have high energy -- Increasing from 80 to 110 or 120.

The focus of your 2nd working set will be on the negative failure portion. Curl explosively, contract slightly for about half a second, and come down slow for 5-7 seconds. As you increase your reps during the set, you'll only be able to come down slowly for about 3-5 seconds, then 1-3 seconds. You conclude when the weight comes down reasonably quickly on you, no longer in control. Refrain from counting your reps and flex after your set. Only focus on the extreme negative movement and keep the tension.

The following working set (3rd set) will be focused on Power, Positive Failure, and Partials movement added. Your only focus is to curl—no need to concentrate on contraction or negative. Increase the weight by about 2-4 levels and knock out as many reps as possible. Once you reach failure, pause at the bottom of the movement while keeping tension and performing partials. Make sure to target 20 reps for those partials. When you finish the set, flex once again.

The 4th and final working set will require a great deal of intuition. You can decide to increase the weight or leave it where it is. You should only be able to perform a few reps for this final set. Ten reps are your maximum. If you easily go past that, then the weight is too light. The 4th set will be your Power set in this pre-exhaust process. Once you struggle with those last reps, you must decide whether to do a drop set (immediately dropping the weight by half and continuing reps); or perform partials. Perform partials if your lower knee area needs a bit of work, or go with the drop set if you want more separation and a great pump. You can also do a drop set with the negative as the primary focus. Once again, coming down slowly for 5-7 seconds. That approach will develop higher-quality muscle tissue. So, you have three options on that 4th set. Whatever feels right in the moment, go with that option. Let's recap the complete process to get a better picture:

1. Stretch then 15 reps at 40 resistance (it can be 30,40,50 or 60).

2. Stretch then 15 reps at 40 resistance

3. Double the weight after warm-up, Feel Set, and Contraction Failure Focus.

4. Increase Weight, Negative Failure Focus

5. Increase Weight, Positive Failure with Partials added.

6. Increase weight; Power Set adding Partials or Drop Set or Drop Set with Negative Failure.

Think of the pre-exhaust process as a journey. Planning or worrying about how heavy you can go or how many reps to do takes away from what will make your muscles grow. Hit failure on the positive, on the negative, and contraction. Then add some power at the end. Cover all your bases. Strength, power increase, muscle separation, and endurance will all happen indirectly.

Chapter 11: Adaptation Principle (Quads Cont.)

Building high-quality, powerful legs as a natural lifter is a challenging task. You must train at higher levels of efficiency to accomplish comparable results to enhanced bodybuilders. I'm using enhanced as a euphemism for what I mean – steroids. Avid lifters fail to realize that you must train under the same conditions to achieve the same results as professionals or famous personalities you see on social media. The truth of what works gets watered down for the sake of constant content creation. What you see online are highlights with filtered workouts that appear exciting and captivating but seldom work. People want excitement and hype instead of something that works. This chapter, combined with the previous one, will help you develop similar, if not better, quads than those portraying filtered training methods. This book's strategies not only work but are extremely practical. An intelligent person often sees these methods' effectiveness within the first few training days and seldom returns to hype.

Excessive barbell squats for 16-20 reps, using every fiber of your being as you push through every set, is not sustainable. Lifting is a lifestyle and a lifelong game. And because of those two reasons, longevity should be your primary focus. You only have one back and one pair of knees. Many young people have permanently injured their backs or knees because of squatting or deadlifting excessively. They think it's cool to squat and don't approach it with respect -- the respect such a powerful training method deserves. Don't be one of those people. Be more intelligent and wiser. The 70+-year-old future you will thank you.

Your quads do not understand weight measurements. They comprehend two things: heavy or not heavy. With pre-exhausting followed by a power workout, we're fooling your quads into thinking the weight is heavier than it is when doing leg presses or squats soon after. Therefore, when you hack squat, leg press, or barbell squat 1 to 2 plates on each side, those plates will feel like 3 or 4. Your quads will think the weight is heavier than it is and adapt accordingly. A similar effect is achieved to those squatting 4 or 5 plates without pre-exhausting targeting an excruciating number of reps. That's what makes the method of pre-exhausting so powerful. Followed by a power movement such as squats or leg presses is just extra. An additional benefit to pre-exhausting followed by a power movement is a lesser toll on the lower back because there is less strain due to the lighter weight. Still, your quads won't know the difference.

Let's say you just accomplished a fantastic pre-exhaust. Your quads are pumped to an extreme. You feel good! While you think about how good you feel, proceed to your favorite power-based quad workout. My preference is hack squats for my first option, followed by leg press as my second option, then regular barbell squats as my third. If hack squats are taken, I proceed with leg press; if the leg press machine is taken, I proceed with regular squats.

HACK SQUAT

Option #1 for Adaptation

Option #2 for Adaptation

Option #3 for Adaptation

Let's assume we share the same preference and proceed with hack squats. You approach the workout with the mindset of control, power, and adaptation. You remind yourself to discard the general approach of pushing yourself for excruciating reps and breaking some record. You already pushed yourself during your pre-exhaust session as you accomplished all levels of failure. So doing the same thing here would be redundant. What would be the point? Let's proceed to what each set will look like for your power movement using hack squats as our example:

Set #1:

- I begin by adding a 45lb plate on each side, but you may start with 10's, 25's, or 35's to begin your first set in pursuit of quad adaptation.

- This first set doubles as a "feel" and a negatively focused set.

- Your target is 10 reps. No more, no less.

- Initiate the movement going slow on the negative-- all the way down for 5 seconds; strive for a full-range movement. Get an excellent stretch.

- Push up explosively and repeat the process until you get to 10 reps. Stop at ten reps, even if you can do a lot more.

- Rest for 1-2 minutes as you mentally prepare for your second set.

Set #2:

- For your second set, double the weight to two plates on each side

- Proceed with 5 well-controlled reps. Rest for 1-2 minutes as you prepare for your third set.

Set #3:

- For your third set, triple the weight to three plates on each side

- Proceed with 3 reps.

- At this point you are entering something I call The Critical Range. You can stop after your third set or add more weight to do a 4th set for one rep.

Set #4:

- For your fourth set, quadruple the weight to four plates on each side

- Proceed with 1 rep only

Set #5:

- Add slightly more weight. You can add 5lbs on each side, 10lbs, 15lbs, or whatever you want.

- Proceed with 1 rep only.

- DO NOT GO PAST 5 SETS

Intuition is required after that fourth set because a mental fatigue element may occur. Finishing at the fourth set might be the wisest move. Because if you achieve that mental fatigue during the fifth quad adaptation set, your hamstring and calve workout might be less intense and focused. YOU must make that determination after your third set. Decide if you will do as many reps as possible during your fourth set or go beyond to a fifth set. Tackle the fifth set if you feel highly invigorated with lots of energy and motivation. If you don't, move on to hamstrings and use the power you would have used on that fifth set and apply it to them. When approaching adaptation, you may use the following to guide you as you begin your new process:

Level 1: One 10lb plate on each side, two 10lb plates, three 10lb plates, four 10lb plates, and adding slightly more weight for a fifth set.

Level 2: One 25lb plate on each side, two, three, four, and slightly more weight for a 5th set.

Level 3: One 35lb plate on each side, two, three, four, and slightly more weight for a 5th set.

Level 4: One 45lb plate on each side, two, three, four, and slightly more weight for a 5th set.

Level 5+: Follow the same pattern as previous levels and adjust as needed.

Make sure to reserve the mental, physical, and motivational energy to properly work those hamstrings and calves. You might decide only to perform three sets for the power movement. That's absolutely a good decision. Sometimes I do three, and sometimes I go for five sets. You want to go all out as a whole. Thinking to yourself, "Is there a benefit in accomplishing another set?" Remember the purpose of the power movement after pre-exhausting. The objective is for your quads to adapt to the stimulus rather than going for an absurd amount of reps. You accomplished that already during the pre-exhaust portion. There's a balance to be kept at all times. Balance is an excellent concept to apply during every workout. Pre-exhausting and adaptation will take your quads to a whole other level. Improve on the method if possible, but make sure to maintain the core principles.

Chapter 12: Hamstring Optimization

Hamstrings tend to be challenging to develop because of the tools available to train them. Squats will do the trick if you have a genetic inclination for superior leg development. But most of us do not share this advantage. Therefore, incredible hamstrings seem out of reach. You bought this book because you need more than standard or trendy methods. You give it your all every rep and every set in hopes that one day your hamstrings will catch up with your efforts. Unfortunately, hamstrings are stubborn muscles where hard work and effort seldom pay off. Strategy, focus, and being smarter will get you superior results, not sheer effort.

Some people have naturally powerful legs without the size to justify such power. And some fail to grow no matter what they do. I fall under the category of having naturally powerful legs with a challenging time getting the size to match my strength level. Living by power, strength, and countless reps is not always the solution. Some finesse is occasionally required.

Isolating as much as possible is vital when a lack of development dilemma persists. You must become a master of isolation – with an emphasis on focus. Some machines break this focus and isolation emphasis instantly because of their design -- the seated hamstring curl machine comes to mind as a machine with less-than-ideal benefit. That machine's design facilitates an unstable pulling movement instead of a curling motion hamstrings require. An undesired outcome of the pulling motion is constant lower-back tightness due to instability. Refrain from using the seated hamstring curl machine if possible.

SEATED HAMSTRING CURLS

AVOID

- Lower Back Tightness
- Unstable
- Pulling Motion
- Innefective

The prone hamstring machine (where you lay face down) also has intricacies. Simply laying down and performing reps until you feel a nice burn won't cut it. Focused and unique methods are required, such as constant contraction for long periods and negative centric movements. But those need to be at a higher weight level. Once again, lower back tightness may occur as you attempt to get into those heavier sets – heavier sets required for growth. You see the dilemma here. Lower back tightness may also occur.

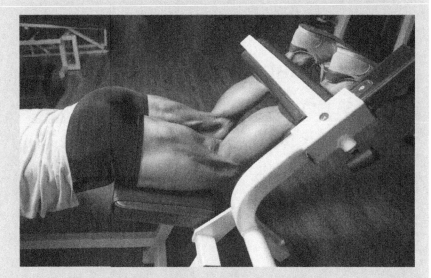

PRONE HAMSTRING CURLS

- Most Common at Gyms
- Ideal for Individual Leg Tempo Method
- Our Example

One way to solve the lower back tightness issue is to perform the same workout with each leg individually. Because the weight is lighter, the body has superior stability overall. You must realize that 160lbs on both legs is different from 80lbs for one leg. On the one hand, you have 160lbs weighing you down, and on the other hand, you have 80lbs weighing you down. Besides being weighed down to a lesser degree for greater stability, there is another massive advantage to single-leg training. The advantage is hamstring size symmetry and balance. When you curl your hamstrings with both legs, your dominant leg tends to take over even if you're highly skilled at proper control. Neither leg will grow because the dominant leg will get fatigued from taking over the movement, not giving it the stimulus for shock and growth. And your non-dominant leg won't get any worthwhile work because of your dominant leg taking over.

So, let's say you are attempting to hamstring curl 160lbs on the prone machine. You might not notice initially, but your dominant leg pulls 100lbs while your weaker leg pulls 60lbs. This imbalance becomes more apparent as your hamstrings become more fatigued.

Your dominant leg will want to take over more and more as the sets, reps, and weight increase. Training with one leg at a time, beginning with your weaker, non-dominant leg first, maintains greater balance, stability, power, control, and overall symmetry.

Now that you know the why let's move on to the how. To begin, we must warm up with two sets, a similar process to the Quad extension pre-exhaustion from Chapter 1. Your two warm-up sets will start with your weaker, non-dominant leg. Even if you're strong, maintain a warm-up range of 10 resistance to 30 resistance. Perform 10 reps while ensuring your ankle is aligned with your hamstring as you curl. Some people tend to curl inward towards their butt. And others tend to curl outward toward their hip. Keep the angle perfectly aligned. On Chapter 8, a similar concept is used for the arm biceps. The concept is based on keeping the wrist directly aligned with the bicep for maximum contraction and development, with absolutely zero movements by the wrist. Use the same notion here by keeping the ankle aligned with the hamstring.

Once you do 10 reps with your weaker non-dominant leg (the left leg for most people), switch to the dominant leg and match the reps for 10. For your second warm-up set, you may increase the weight by one level or keep it at the current level. Then, repeat the process by curling with your weaker leg, then your stronger leg. After you finish warming up, our next task is to target five exceptionally effective sets.

Exceptionally effective sets require a higher level of focus. Shift your mindset away from the effort-driven perspective you would use for other more effort-intensive movements. There is a key tempo I will teach you to facilitate this process and make every hamstring set an achievement. You will feel every rep and set counts with an indescribable peace of mind.

Tempo Process (First Set Example):

1) After warming up, increase the weight by one level.

2) Lay down and Begin with your weaker leg

3) Curl, then hold the contraction at the top of the movement for two seconds -- counting ("One, Two") in your head. Make sure to squeeze towards you with purpose!

4) Come down slow for three seconds on the negative – Counting ("One, Two, Three") in your head as you come down.

5) Then count "One" when you finish the rep back at the starting position.

6) Repeat for rep 2 with "One, Two" on contraction, "One, Two, Three" on the negative, and "Two" for completion at starting position.

7) Continue with the same method until failure.

8) Switch Legs and repeat while matching the rep count. If you performed 10 reps to failure on your non-dominant leg, then match the count with your dominant leg. Do not exceed it.

The exciting part about the tempo process is your brain's subsequent adaptation. After the first few weeks of practice, it will be natural. You won't need to count on the contraction or negative portions every set. You might count the tempo during your first set; then, you'll maintain the rhythm naturally every following set and only focus on matching the rep count. You'll be able to perform each rep with the same rhythm without even thinking about it. Rep count will be your only focus once you hone in with precision. Tempo count will become innate. And with enough practice, you'll be able to change your tempo to any count you desire and adapt much quicker to add variation. For now, please stick to the rhythm in the example provided because it is the most effective for muscle growth. Try out different tempos and see for yourself. Now let's proceed with the five sets that are most optimal to achieve superior results:

Warm-Up Set #1: 10 reps with left leg, then 10 reps with right leg at 10lb resistance.

Warm-Up Set #2: 10 reps with left leg, then 10 reps with right leg at 20lb resistance.

Set #1: Failure with left leg, then match the number of reps with the right leg, two-second contraction squeeze, and three-second negative control for each rep at 20lb resistance.

Set #2: Failure with left leg, then match the number with right leg, two-second contraction squeeze, and three-second negative control for each rep at 30lb resistance.

Set #3: Failure with left leg, then match the number with right leg, two-second contraction squeeze, and three-second negative control for each rep at 40lb resistance.

Set #4: Failure with left leg, then match the number with right leg, two-second contraction squeeze, and three-second negative control for each rep at 50lb resistance.

Set #5 With Drop Set Added: Failure with left leg, then match the number with right leg, two-second contraction squeeze, and three-second negative control for each rep at 60lb resistance – quickly drop weight to 30lb resistance, do as many quick reps as possible with your left leg with no tempo, then match number of reps with your right leg.

That's just an example of the process. I understand endurance and strength levels will vary by individual. Some simple adjustments can easily be made according to your endurance and strength level. Progressively loading the weight is optional. You may also strip the weight and lower it level by level after reaching a point where it is too heavy to perform a proper rep. The following example addresses such a dilemma with a process almost identical to what I previously described. But with a couple of simple adjustments after **Set #3:**

Warm-Up Set #1: 10lb resistance.

Warm-Up Set #2: 20lb resistance.

Set #1: 20lb resistance to failure each leg following tempo.

Set #2: 30lb resistance to failure for each leg following tempo.

Set #3: 40lb resistance to failure for each leg following tempo—You soon realize the weight starts getting too heavy for a proper rep, proper contraction, or proper negative control.

Set #4: Lower the weight to 30lb resistance and proceed to failure following tempo.

Set #5: With Drop Set Added Quickly: Failure with left leg, then match the number with right leg, two-second contraction squeeze, and three-second negative control for each rep at _20lb resistance_ – quickly drop weight to _10lb resistance_, do as many quick reps as possible with your left leg with no tempo, then match number of reps with your right leg.

Making those adjustments is necessary for the hamstrings to develop to higher levels. If you're reasonably strong with a lot of endurance, your pattern, including two warm-up sets, might be 20lb, 30lb, 50lb, 60lb, 70lb, 80lb, and 90lb with a 40lb drop set added quickly. You can adjust the patterns according to your strength and endurance levels.

Note: You can use the standing hamstring curl machine also and follow this process. It is exactly the same, but the machine is less common. That's why I used the prone hamstring machine as an example.

STANDING HAMSTRING CURLS

- Less Common at Gyms
- Great Alternative to Prone
- Will Work Just as Good If Not Better Than Prone

When lifters find a routine or process they enjoy, they exhaust it until it stops working. Even I'm guilty of this. If I find some method I enjoy that works very well, I stick to it with the same type of reps, rhythm, pattern, or tempo. You need to be aware of this to break free from it. Changing it up into workouts or training methods that are not effective is not an intelligent way to seek a variation. Please stick to the structure of this tempo-based hamstring training, but add variations to it once you master the two-second contraction with a three-second negative. Here are some variations for you to consider. These variations will open your mind to new possibilities where growth and motivation are constant.:

- Slow curl, two-second contraction, three-second negative
- Quick/explosive curl, two-second contraction, three-second negative
- Quick/explosive curl, one-second contraction, four-second negative
- Slow curl, one-second contraction, four-second negative.
- Quick/explosive curl, five-second contraction (on lighter weight) five second negative.
- Slow curl, five-second contraction (on lighter weight), five-second negative.

Your creativity will determine how you wish to approach this masterful approach. For example, you may decide to hold a five-second contraction the lighter the weight. Then lower the contraction after every set to four seconds, three seconds, two seconds, and one second the heavier it gets. The possibilities are endless once individual leg tempo training becomes innate.

So, what about resting between sets? Your rest should be 15-30 seconds between sets because you work each leg individually. One leg is resting while you work on the other so you can seamlessly begin your next set as soon as you want. Taking a breather between sets is ideal. 15-30 seconds will work. Anything beyond that is a waste of time. You will rest the same amount of time as if you were training both legs, requiring 1-2 minutes of rest. Training each leg individually should not take longer than training both simultaneously. This hamstring optimization process is more effective and requires a higher level of focus. How sharp your focus becomes as you practice day in and day out will determine your gains. Perfect the form. Perfect the process. Get creative with your tempo variations once you adapt to an effective one. Focus on the

process with precision, and growth will be inevitable.

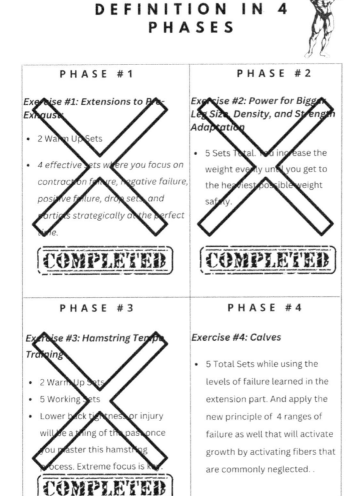

MAX SIZE & DEFINITION IN 4 PHASES

PHASE #1

Exercise #1: Extensions to Pre-Exhaust.

- 2 Warm Up Sets

- *4 effective sets where you focus on contraction failure, negative failure, positive failure, drop sets, and partials strategically at the perfect time.*

COMPLETED

PHASE #2

Exercise #2: Power for Bigger Leg Size, Density, and Strength Adaptation

- 5 Sets Total. You increase the weight evenly until you get to the heaviest possible weight safely.

COMPLETED

PHASE #3

Exercise #3: Hamstring Tempo Training

- 2 Warm Up Sets
- 5 Working Sets
- Lower back tightness or injury will be a thing of the past once you master this hamstring process. Extreme focus is key.

COMPLETED

PHASE #4

Exercise #4: Calves

- 5 Total Sets while using the levels of failure learned in the extension part. And apply the new principle of 4 ranges of failure as well that will activate growth by activating fibers that are commonly neglected. .

Chapter 13: Mental Game for Calves

Lifting is the only area of life where failure can have a positive outcome. You want to fail and need to fail every set. This chapter will give you keen insight into ideal ways of taking your muscles to failure. Yes, this chapter is no calves, but you can apply the concepts to all other muscles you wish to train. Failure is more complex than pushing those reps beyond a pain threshold. Pumping reps non-stop where your muscles give out is only failing on the Positive.

Most people only focus on pushing or pulling movements, making it their mission to increase personal records for strength. They think the workout was an accomplishment if they increased their leg press, squat, hamstring curls, or calf raises by a few pounds or kilograms. Unfortunately, playing that mental game will only give you short-term progress. A surefire way of consistently breaking personal records, without worrying about breaking personal records, is to reach failure on three levels: positive movement, negative movement, and contraction. Focusing on those three levels of failure were first conceived by Six consecutive times Mr. Olympia English Champion Dorian Yates – arguably one of the greatest bodybuilders of his era and a genius at the craft.

This book is taking what already exists and improving it for ultimate efficiency, cutting out the noise and familiar wasted movements or sets. This book has shown you how to reach failure on all three levels. But this book also offers a hidden gem most lifters overlook or never use. The hidden gem is the fourth level of failure. That fourth level of failure is something I like to call Stretch Fatigue. Calves respond exceptionally well to that fourth level of failure. Stretch fatigue isn't the only groundbreaking strategy you'll be learning; you'll also know how to fail on four ranges for calves. Combining Stretch Fatigue and four ranges with three failure levels is a new tier of training. These new concepts should not overwhelm you or intimidate you whatsoever. Please enjoy the process as I teach

you how to apply them simply for continued growth and size.

Going heavy isn't always ideal for developing muscle quality and

size. Adding at least one heavy set to your process for each muscle

group can be beneficial, but more needs to happen. For most muscle

levels of failure, pushing as close to 5 reps as possible after it starts

burning and going heavy should do the trick to stimulate growth and quality. Calves, however, are a bit more sophisticated. An excessive number of reps and constant contraction assist in their development, and adding stretch fatigue will almost ensure it. This method will improve the overall quality and aesthetic if you have great calves genetically. And if you don't, the process will ensure you break that genetic barrier and build the calves you've always wanted. These are the steps to optimize The Four Levels of failure properly:

Step #1: Start from the bottom, getting a full stretch on the calves for 5 seconds. Impose your will on it.

Step #2: Raise explosively and hold the contraction for 2 seconds. Impose your will on it. Contract hard!

Step #3: Come Down slowly for three seconds of negative focus.

Step #4: Repeat the process for many reps without counting them. Focus on a 5-second stretch, raise explosively/quickly, hold the 2-second contraction, and come down slowly with a 3-second negative.

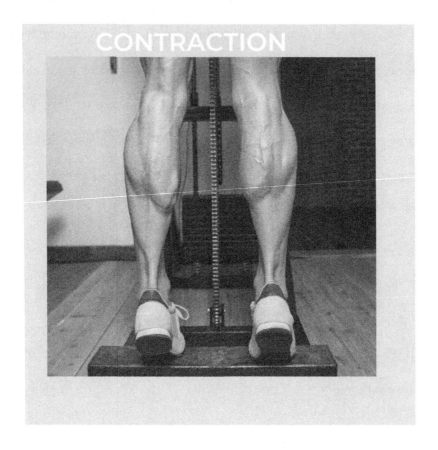

I often see lifters performing reps up and down, adding weight with zero focus on contraction, negative, or stretch. Unfortunately, training in that manner does very little. Calves are special. They require a lot of effort with a simplified focus on the steps I previously described. In addition, the stretch fatigue component will ensure your calves get tired much quicker while stimulating growth. These are all practical things to remember that can also be applied to other muscle groups. Failing on The Four Ranges for calves is similar to the method of doing partials but slightly more intricate in the focus department. However, the whole process is straightforward. It is completed in one set without any rest. These are the steps:

Step #1: Perform as many reps as possible from the stretch position and raise to the contraction position until you can't do anymore -- complete failure. Don't hold the contraction at all. Just do the reps quickly.

Step #2: Without rest, continue from the stretch position and raise only halfway for as many reps as possible until you can't continue pushing halfway anymore.

Step #3: Without rest, continue from the stretch position 1/4 of the way until you reach failure.

Step #4: From the stretch position, only raise slightly with your calves barely moving until failure. You will only be raising a few centimeters from the stretch position.

Make sure to stagger each method for your five sets. For example, the first set will be focused on The Four Levels of failure, and the second set will be focused on The Four Ranges of failure for calves. For each workout, you can change the pattern. Here's an example of your sets

Set #1: Fatigue stretch for 5 seconds, Raise quickly and hold the contraction for 2 seconds; go down slowly with a 3-second negative back to the starting position (the stretch).

Set #2: Quick reps full range until failure, without rest, continue with quick reps halfway, without rest, continue with quick reps 1/4 of the way, without rest, continue pushing slightly from the stretch position for just a few centimeters.

Set #3: Repeat Set #1

Set #4: Repeat Set #2

Set #5: Choose between Set #1 or #2 to finish off—your choice.

Keep the structure every time you train. If you want to add variation, then you can change how long you contract, how long you stretch fatigue, and how fast you raise. Changing the rhythm by changing the timing will ensure your muscles remain confused once they get used to the stimulus. Give your muscles time to adapt, then change the timing. Try the process with no weight at first. Then, add weight to your raises when your calves get more powerful and develop higher endurance. Eventually, you'll master the process to an unbelievable level -- and your calves will visually manifest your mastery.

WEIGHTLIFTING TO GROW MUSCLE - UNITED KINGDOM

Chapter 14: Lower-Back, Abs, and Additional Tips

Your pursuit of amazing abs should be a fun-filled journey. I'm not a fan of having a routine regarding abs. However, our whole leg training process will enhance your core strength. In addition, your lower back and your abs will be indirectly strengthened by completing everything we just covered. Those additional benefits of our leg development process ensure you save time training your lower back and doing abs. You only need 1 set for the lower back. Yes! Only one set. There is no trick to it or anything. Performing one set for lower back extensions will do the trick. Do as many reps for lower back extensions as possible once you complete calves and you're done.

Abs are a luxury. Research and find 2-minute ab workouts online that you can perform once you finish your lower back extensions. Find a different workout each time you train your legs. Find something simple and quick. You already won the day after completing this extensive leg process. Spend about 5 minutes between your lower back extension set, your 2-minute ab workout, and stretching.

Here are some additional tips:

Tip #1: You don't have to all levels of failure in one set. You can split the levels of failure into different sets. For example, you can focus on failing on the positive on set one, then focus on failing on the negative on set 2, then focus on failing on contraction on set three, then fail on all levels on set 4.

Tip #2: Keep your feet and legs shoulder width apart when training your legs. Putting your feet close, wide, or awkward angles will cause knee injury eventually. Weird angles and weird positions will get you injured. Maintain a natural alignment.

Tip #3: Every 3 weeks make sure to skip the Power for Adaptation Phase for quads. Give your hips extra healing time and your lower back. Instead, add those 5 sets to leg extensions. Your leg extension workout will be 10 sets. It also ensures your master ways to reach failure more effectively during extensions with a more extended extension training.

Tip #4: Shifting Phase #2 and Phase #3 is also a good idea. It will greatly shock your muscles once you get used to the process and master it. But only after you master it after months of training.

S H I F T
P H A S E # 2 & # 3

PHASE #1	PHASE #2
Exercise #1: Extensions to Pre-Exhaust: • 2 Warm Up Sets • *4 effective sets where you focus on contraction failure, negative failure, positive failure, drop sets, and partials strategically at the perfect time.*	**Exercise #2: Hamstring Tempo Training** • 2 Warm Up Sets • 5 Working Sets • Lower back tightness or injury will be a thing of the past once you master this hamstring process. Extreme focus is key.
PHASE #3	PHASE #4
Exercise #3: Power for Bigger Leg Size, Density, and Strength Adaptation • 5 Sets Total. You increase the weight evenly until you get to the heaviest possible weight safely.	**Exercise #4: Calves** • 5 Total Sets while using the levels of failure learned in the extension part. And apply the new principle of 4 ranges of failure as well that will activate growth by activating fibers that are commonly neglected. .

SKIPPING POWER PHASE FOR EXTRA HIP AND LOWER BACK RECOVERY

PHASE #1	PHASE #2
Exercise #1: Extensions to Pre-Exhaust:	*Exercise #2: Hamstring Tempo Training*
• 2 Warm Up Sets • *8-10 effective sets where you focus on contraction failure, negative failure, positive failure, drop sets, and partials strategically at the perfect time.*	• 2 Warm Up Sets • 5 Working Sets • Lower back tightness or injury will be a thing of the past once you master this hamstring process. Extreme focus is key.

PHASE #3

Exercise #3: Calves

• 5 Total Sets while using the levels of failure learned in the extension part. And apply the new principle of 4 ranges of failure as well that will activate growth by activating fibers that are commonly neglected. .

Last Thoughts: Thank you very much for purchasing this book. Continue to evolve your methods and the way you train. Please, rate and review this book when you have the time. It helps tremendously. Doing so allows me to sell more books. The more books I sell, the more I can write and bring your more advanced training methods that go beyond this book. I'm already working on one that's exceptionally advanced, and knowing if I'm on the right track to provide you with something outstanding is highly beneficial. Thank you very much once again. Stay strong!